CAMPAIGN 405

MERS EL-KÉBIR 1940

Operation *Catapult*

RYAN K. NOPPEN   ILLUSTRATED BY ADAM TOOBY

OSPREY PUBLISHING
Bloomsbury Publishing Plc
Kemp House, Chawley Park, Cumnor Hill, Oxford OX2 9PH, UK
29 Earlsfort Terrace, Dublin 2, Ireland
1385 Broadway, 5th Floor, New York, NY 10018, USA
E-mail: info@ospreypublishing.com
www.ospreypublishing.com

OSPREY is a trademark of Osprey Publishing Ltd

First published in Great Britain in 2024

A catalogue record for this book is available from the British Library.

ISBN: PB 9781472859709; eBook 9781472859716;
ePDF 9781472859693; XML 9781472859686

24 25 26 27 28   10 9 8 7 6 5 4 3 2 1

Maps by Bounford.com
3D BEVs by Paul Kime
Index by Richard Munro
Typeset by PDQ Digital Media Solutions, Bungay, UK
Printed by Repro India Ltd.

MIX
Paper
FSC   FSC® C047271

Acknowledgements

The author wishes to thank Paul Bevand and Rob White of the HMS Hood
Association for their most generous research assistance. The author also
wishes to thank Pascal Landure-Chosse and Aubry Palouzier of l'Association
Amicale des Anciens Marins de Mers-el-Kébir et des Familles des Victimes
for their help in obtaining unique historical photographs for this work.
Lastly, the author also wishes to thank his lovely wife Sarah, his beautiful
Peanut Emma, and his funny Spud Henry for allowing him the time to write
this work.

Author's Note

All times given are according to British Summer Time (BST).

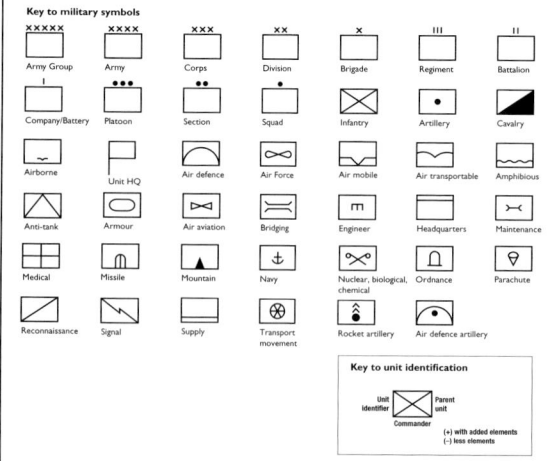

Front cover main illustration: Royal Navy aerial torpedo attack on
Dunkerque, 0655hrs on 6 July 1940. (Adam Tooby)

Title page image: Aerial photograph of the disposition of Amiral Gensoul's
remaining capital ships in Mers el-Kébir harbour on 4 July. (Collection
l'Association Amicale des Anciens Marins de Mers-el-Kébir et des Familles des
Victimes)

CONTENTS

ORIGINS OF THE BATTLE
4

The French collapse ▪ Increasing mistrust among former allies

CHRONOLOGY
20

OPPOSING COMMANDERS
23

British ▪ French

OPPOSING FORCES
29

British ▪ French ▪ Orders of battle

OPPOSING PLANS
34

British ▪ French

THE CAMPAIGN
40

Final negotiations ▪ Mers el-Kébir ▪ Great Britain and Alexandria
The immediate French response ▪ Operation *Lever* and aftermath

AFTERMATH
90

Analysis and conclusion

BIBLIOGRAPHY
94

INDEX
95

ORIGINS OF THE BATTLE

On the late morning of 13 June 1940, a de Havilland Flamingo transport aircraft carefully touched down on the runway – potted with craters due to a recent German aerial bombing – at the airport of Tours, roughly 200km to the south-west of Paris. As the Flamingo's escort of Spitfire fighters touched down around the transport, a portly, elderly gentleman made as dignified of an exit as he could out of the inconveniently small door of the aircraft. The gentleman and his party looked around; no one was there to meet him, and no one had bothered to send a car to pick him up. This was hardly the sort of reception expected for a visiting head of state, but to Winston Churchill, it showed just how desperate and chaotic the situation was on the ground in France. As Churchill arrived in Tours, several German armies were rapidly nearing the outskirts of Paris, having breached the hastily assembled Weygand Line along the Rivers Somme and Aisne. The French government had abandoned Paris on 11 June and declared it an open city. On 10 June, Italy had declared war on the Allies, and with all fronts seemingly collapsing, commandant en chef de l'armée française (Commander-in-Chief of the French Army) Général Maxime Weygand insisted to président du Conseil des ministres (Prime Minister) Paul Reynaud that the government seek an armistice with the Germans. It was Weygand's rumblings of an armistice that compelled Churchill to make this dangerous and eleventh-hour journey to France, to bolster the morale of his desolate French counterpart; France had to be kept in the fight.

After borrowing a staff car from the airfield commander, Churchill and his aides drove into the city and eventually managed to rendezvous with Reynaud at the Préfecture de Tours, the temporary seat of the French government, later that afternoon. The meeting was not an encouraging one for Churchill; despondent, Reynaud asked what the British reaction would be to the French seeking an armistice. Reynaud was referring to a resolution, adopted at the 28 March 1940 meeting of the Anglo-French Supreme War Council, which stated that during the present conflict neither France nor Great Britain would negotiate or conclude an armistice or peace treaty without the consent of the other. Churchill stated that he was sympathetic to the French plight, but that Great Britain expected its ally to fight on, even if the French government and armed forces had to withdraw to its colonies in North Africa. Reynaud countered that France alone could do no more and its successful participation in the war could only continue if the United States joined the Allied cause – an eventuality that both Churchill and Reynaud had unsuccessfully sought since the beginning of the conflict. Nothing more of any substance was said at the meeting and both sides adjourned, having failed to agree on a united course of action.

There was one French officer noticeably missing from the meeting at the Préfecture, likely the one Churchill was most eager to buoy as well as receive assurances from: Chef d'état-major de la Marine (Chief of Staff of the French Navy) Amiral François Darlan of the Marine Nationale Française (French Navy). Churchill had been in France a day earlier for a meeting of the Anglo-French Supreme War Council at the Château du Muguet near Briare, roughly 130km south of Paris. At this meeting, Reynaud was not as pessimistic of France's military situation as he was a day later, but Churchill heard Général Weygand's dire appraisal of conditions on the ground and his recommendation that France seek an armistice. The French Army capitulating to the Germans would not have immediate consequences for the survival of the British Empire in the conflict, but the capitulation of the French Navy might.

Prime Minister Winston Churchill exiting a de Havilland DH.95 Flamingo transport. (Author's collection)

The greatest fear in Churchill's mind regarding a French armistice was the possibility of Germany assuming control over the vessels of the fourth-largest navy in the world, a scenario – in Churchill's mind – in which Great Britain could lose control of its seaborne connections with its empire. At the end of the conference on 12 June, Churchill addressed this very concern with Amiral Darlan, insisting that the French fleet never fall into German hands; Darlan solemnly promised that he would not allow it to happen. As Churchill flew back to London following the 13 June meeting at Tours, the Prime Minister wondered if Darlan's resolve may have changed overnight, as had Reynaud's, and he had not had the opportunity to question the admiral; Darlan was in Bordeaux, setting up a new naval headquarters. Doubt crept into Churchill's mind and would fester in the coming days. This doubt, and the uncertainty of French intentions as France tried to extricate itself from a war for survival in which Great Britain would now find itself alone, would rapidly become the catalyst for a violent rupture in Anglo-French relations which no combatant – British, French, German, or Italian – could have foreseen.

Churchill saying farewell to président du Conseil des ministres (Prime Minister) Paul Reynaud after a meeting in Paris, 1 June 1940. (ullstein bild via Getty Images)

THE FRENCH COLLAPSE

After a restless night pondering the possibility of the French withdrawal from the conflict, Churchill woke to the news of a reassuring development on the morning of 14 June. In the predawn hours, Darlan had launched Operation *Vado*, a bombardment of strategic targets along Italy's Ligurian coast with the cruisers and destroyers of the Marine Nationale's 3ème Escadre, based in Toulon. Vice-Amiral Émile Duplat sent the heavy cruisers *Algérie* and *Foch* and six destroyers to bombard oil storage tanks in Vado Ligure and a steel

French heavy cruiser *Algérie*, photographed in Toulon in 1939. *Algérie*, with Vice-Amiral Émile Duplat flying his flag aboard, led the vessels of the Marine Nationale's 3ème Escadre in a raid against the north-western Italian coast during Operation *Vado* on 13–14 June 1940. (Roger Viollet via Getty Images)

works in Savona, while he ordered the light cruisers *Colbert* and *Dupleix* and five destroyers to attack harbour facilities around Genoa. While the damage inflicted was minimal, it demonstrated to Churchill that the Marine Nationale, and its commander, still possessed the willingness to take the fight to the enemy. Having longed for years to take the fight to the Italians, Darlan fully committed the Marine Nationale to offensive operations in the Mediterranean in the week following this opening bombardment. French submarines, operating out of Bizerte in Tunisia, set up a patrol line across the central Mediterranean and several conducted minelaying operations off the Italian coast.

Since the end of May, the Marine Nationale had stationed a squadron in the eastern Mediterranean to assist the British Mediterranean Fleet – Force X, composed of the modernized dreadnought battleship *Lorraine*, heavy cruisers *Duquesne*, *Suffren*, and *Tourville*, light cruiser *Duguay-Trouin*, destroyers *Basque*, *Forbin*, and *Fortuné*, and submarine *Protée*, all under the command of Vice-Amiral René-Émile Godfroy. On 11 June, Godfroy departed Beirut with his cruisers and destroyers to patrol the waters around Italy's Dodecanese Islands in the Southern Aegean, serving as a diversion from Operation *Vado* in the west and to deter any potential moves by the Regia Marina (Royal Italian Navy) in the eastern Mediterranean. Five submarines based in Beirut also took up patrol stations throughout the Dodecanese. On 14 June, Godfroy took Force X to Alexandria to rendezvous with the Mediterranean Fleet, commanded by Vice Admiral Sir Andrew Cunningham.

The situation for French naval units in northern and western France was much different during the days of the Mediterranean offensive operations, however. On 13 June, German ground forces breached French defensive lines along the Rivers Seine and Marne, and Paris fell to the Wehrmacht the following day. At that time the German XV.Armee-Korps, under the command of General der Infanterie Hermann Hoth, began a rapid drive across Normandy. In the coming days, Hoth sent the 7. Panzerdivision, under Generalmajor Erwin Rommel, towards the Cotentin Peninsula to capture the naval base at Cherbourg while the 5. Panzerdivision, under General der Panzertruppen Joachim Lemelsen, was ordered to drive across Brittany and seize the Marine Nationale's primary Atlantic base in the port of Brest. With French ground forces unable to stem this renewed German advance, Lieutenant-General Alan Brooke, commander of the remaining BEF units in France, recommended to Churchill the withdrawal of all British troops from north-western France on the evening of 14 June, to which the Prime Minister readily agreed.

On the following day, the British launched Operation *Aerial*, the evacuation of all British troops from France. British troops began to flood into the Atlantic coast ports, clearly displaying to French naval commanders just how dire the situation was. Darlan ordered the commanders in these ports to put up whatever defence they could to buy time for the British evacuation and for the evacuation of all vessels able to put to sea as well as whatever essential ammunition, spare parts, and personnel could be carried. On 15 June, Darlan also told his deputy, Vice-Amiral Maurice Le Luc, that he had no intention of obeying any potential government order to turn over vessels of the Marine Nationale to the Axis as part of an armistice agreement. Darlan then ordered that all Marine Nationale vessels in areas of Metropolitan France threatened by German ground forces should make preparations to immediately evacuate to French colonial or British ports. The fact that vessels were directed both to British and French colonial ports demonstrated that, as late as 15 June, Darlan intended that the Marine Nationale was to fight on alongside its British ally despite the desperate situation in Normandy and Brittany. The morale of the Marine Nationale was high and, unlike the French Army, it had suffered no catastrophic defeats in the field.

While the initiative demonstrated by Darlan on 13–15 June gave brief encouragement to Churchill and the British Admiralty, this was abruptly undercut by the actions of French politicians beginning on 15 June. A growing majority within the French government during these hectic days had turned their ears to Général Weygand's call for an immediate armistice, due in large part to the rapidity of the renewed German advance. Intense pressure from the Council of Ministers compelled Reynaud to ask the British government on 15 June if the French government could inquire of armistice terms from Germany, as Reynaud had just that day received a message from President Franklin D. Roosevelt that the United States was not currently in a position to enter the war. At the time, Reynaud was still discussing the possibility of forming a government in North Africa, which would continue the war against the Axis from the French Empire and, understanding that Reynaud would likely be forced to resign if he opposed the Council of Ministers, Churchill reluctantly agreed to support his French counterpart's request on the following day in an effort to keep him in power. The French government would be allowed to inquire about armistice terms on the strict condition that vessels of the Marine Nationale immediately sail for British ports and that any armistice terms be immediately shared with the British government. A final armistice agreement would have to be approved by the British government, which still held any French government to the terms of the 28 March Unity Declaration.

Having agreed to this concession, Churchill's mind immediately returned to the fate of the French fleet. He was particularly fixated on the fate of the new French battleships, convinced that if they fell into German hands, they would tip the balance of the naval war against the British once Germany's new Bismarck-class battleships entered service. Some senior British naval

The Marine Nationale's offensive spirit in the Mediterranean in mid-June 1940 extended to the skies as well. The Aéronavale's Farman F.223.4 four-engine bomber *Jules Verne*, which famously conducted the first Allied air raid on Berlin on the night of 7 June 1940, was sent on bombing raids over Venice and Livorno on the nights of 13 and 14 June in conjunction with Operation *Vado*, as well as dropping propaganda leaflets over Rome on each return flight. (Author's collection)

French battleship *Strasbourg*. As the most modern French battleships that were operational in June 1940, the fates of *Strasbourg*, and her sister *Dunkerque*, attracted Churchill's immediate attention when France began armistice negotiations with the Axis. (Author's collection)

commanders were not convinced that this scenario was a likely eventuality, but Churchill frequently made his own sweeping naval assessments, not always relying upon the expertise of his admirals. At the Prime Minister's prompting, the Admiralty began making requests on 15 June for the French battleships *Richelieu* and *Jean Bart* to be transferred to British ports; the Royal Navy would provide necessary tugs and escorts. The Admiralty also requested that the Force de Raid – a French squadron made up of the modern battleships *Dunkerque* and *Strasbourg*, the modernized dreadnought battleships *Bretagne* and *Provence*, and several modern destroyers, currently based near Oran in North Africa – be transferred to Gibraltar. That same day, Admiral Cunningham, Commander-in-Chief, Mediterranean at Alexandria, and Vice Admiral Dudley North, Commander-in-Chief, North Atlantic at Gibraltar, both received a message from the Admiralty, originating from Churchill, stating that if *Dunkerque* and *Strasbourg* were not transferred to Gibraltar and there was a threat of their falling into Axis hands, then either admiral might be tasked with their destruction. This was one of the first official suggestions of aggressive action against the warships of the Allied French and it clearly demonstrated Churchill's obsessive concern over the French capital ships.

At this eleventh hour, Churchill also shared with his War Cabinet his intension to offer the French a proposal for the creation of an Anglo-French Union – a single British–French state, with a joint parliament and war cabinet, committed to continuing the war against the Axis – as a last-ditch effort to bolster Reynaud against the defeatist elements in his government. The War Cabinet reluctantly agreed to offer this proposal. Just after Reynaud had received the British government's conditions for pursuing talks of an armistice, he received the details of the proposed Anglo-French Union and enthusiastically took it to the Cabinet of Ministers, hoping to persuade a majority of members to continue the war from France's overseas colonies. The proposal was met with vociferous criticism and ridicule by the armistice faction in the Cabinet of Ministers, however. Unknown to Reynaud, his phone lines had been tapped by French Army intelligence, allowing Weygand to learn of the proposal and thus allowing his ministerial allies time to prepare a concerted attack against it. The proposal was not voted upon, and that evening Reynaud resigned from office, collapsing his government. Retired maréchal de France Philippe Pétain, who was made Deputy Prime Minister by Reynaud's government on 18 May 1940 in an effort to increase French military and political morale, was asked to form a new government and to seek armistice terms from Germany. It is important to note here that before resigning, Reynaud had mentioned the British government's message, allowing the French government to inquire of armistice terms from the Axis, but did not tell the Council of Ministers of the requirement to relocate the vessels of the Marine Nationale to British ports or to immediately inform the British government of any armistice terms. These conditions had been temporarily placed on hold by the British government in an effort to encourage French approval of the Anglo-French Union. But the British ambassador, due to communications lapses and errors, told Reynaud just before his meeting with the Council of Ministers that these preconditions had been cancelled. Therefore, Reynaud did not share them with the Council or with Pétain.

Almost immediately upon taking power in the early hours of 17 June, the new government of Pétain requested armistice terms from Germany. The British government had not been consulted prior to this action, and as the day wore on it became evident that French warships were not making their way to British ports. Churchill was furious, telling his War Cabinet that Pétain and his ministers had violated the 28 March Unity Declaration and did not abide by his specifically laid out preconditions for armistice negotiations. The British ambassador to France, Sir Ronald Campbell, saw Pétain later that day and requested that French warships be immediately sent to British ports so that the French fleet did not become a factor in the armistice negotiations. The old maréchal denied this request but vaguely responded that the French fleet would be kept out of German hands, and for as long as the negotiations were underway French naval facilities in the path of German armies would be rendered inoperable.

Simultaneously, Darlan, now made Ministre de la Marine (Minister of the Navy) by Pétain in addition to Chef d'état-major de la Marine, made a similar promise to the British naval attaché. Of critical importance, however, Darlan made the decision on 17 June not to send his vessels to British ports unless emergency dictated, and all warships in ports vulnerable to German capture were ordered to make their way to North Africa. Upon learning this, any confidence which Churchill previously had in Darlan immediately evaporated. He wondered what had happened to the dynamic leader who was boldly willing to continue the fight against the Axis; what had caused this about-face? Darlan's initial reason for not sending his vessels to British ports, communicated to the Admiralty, was that most ports in Great Britain were vulnerable to German air attack, whereas North African harbours were free from this threat.

Behind the scenes, there were multiple reasons for Darlan's decision. Now as a member of Pétain's government, Darlan clearly recognized the value that the fate of the French fleet would have in armistice negotiations, particularly with Germany. Its fate might be the only card the French government could play to allow France a degree of independence and to keep the French Empire out of Axis hands. While Darlan continued to promise that he would scuttle his vessels before turning them over to the Axis, if the French fleet were immediately turned over to the British then it could play no beneficial role in armistice negotiations. Darlan also wanted to keep the fleet in French hands due to the perceived threat of Spain entering the war on the side of the Axis. Spain had long-standing ambitions for Morocco

From left to right: commandant en chef de l'armée française (Commander-in-Chief of the French Army) Général Maxime Weygand, sous-secrétaire d'État à la présidence (Undersecretary of State for the Presidency) Paul Badouin, président du Conseil des ministres (Prime Minister) Paul Reynaud, and vice-président du Conseil (Deputy Prime Minister) maréchal de France Philippe Pétain. Both Weygand and Pétain were instrumental in compelling Reynaud to resign and in seeking armistice negotiations with the Axis. (Keystone/Hulton Archive/Getty Images)

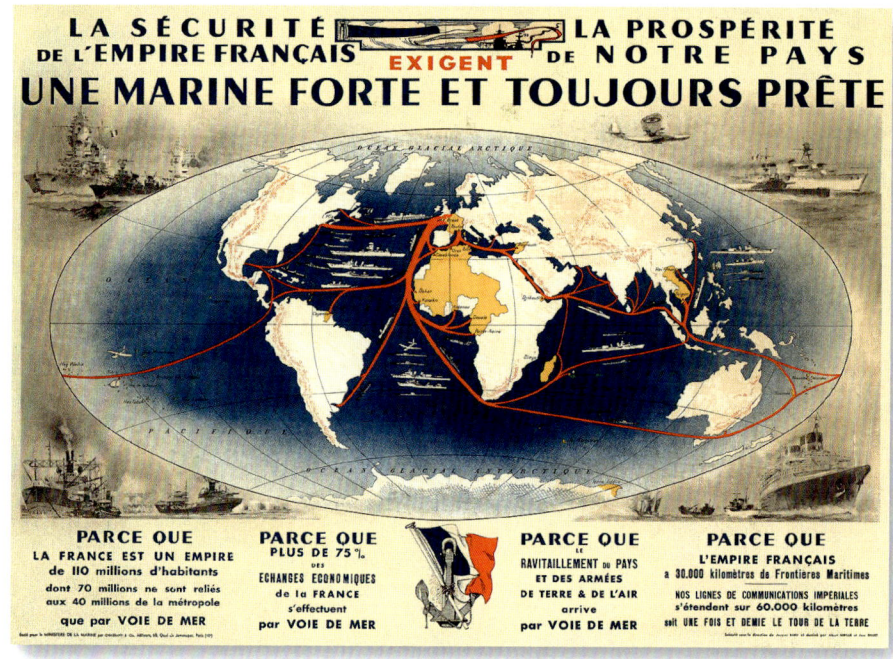

and Darlan knew through his intelligence sources that the Germans were actively courting Spain's *Caudillo*, General Francisco Franco, with offers of French colonial territory for joining the Axis. An intact French fleet could still contain both Italian and Spanish ambitions in the Mediterranean.

Darlan likely had personal reasons for keeping his ships out of British hands. It was well known among Darlan's navy colleagues, and their British contacts, that Darlan regarded the Marine Nationale as his own personal fief, given the wide latitude he had acquired over his command. Politically ambitious or not, he may well have been reluctant to give away not just his command but a modern fleet that he had had a decisive role in constructing. The idea of handing over the fleet that he had built to the British – who in his eyes had prematurely abandoned their commitment to the ground war in France and who were now alone against the Axis, and in his mind unlikely to hold out much longer – was a decision that would not benefit France, and certainly not a decision that would benefit himself. In Darlan's eyes, the French fleet was a French prerogative, not an Allied prerogative, and he was a French admiral who would serve a legitimate government of France – of which he was now a part. The fleet allowed France – and Darlan – independent initiative at a time when its political and military options were increasingly being limited. Finally, rather simply stated but largely true, as with many other French officers and politicians of this time, anti-German sentiments did not equate to pro-British sentiments.

At this critical juncture, both Churchill and Darlan had their own national interests at stake: the survival of the Allied cause, to which the fate of Great Britain and the British Empire was tied, and the survival of France and the French Empire – interests which appeared at the time to be mutually exclusive. Both may have realized and reflected upon this at the time, but their respective desperate fights for survival against the Axis onslaught heightened anxieties and suspicions, which were also shared by their political and military colleagues and subordinates; there was no longer time

The withdrawal of the Marine Nationale from Normandy and Brittany, 17–19 June 1940

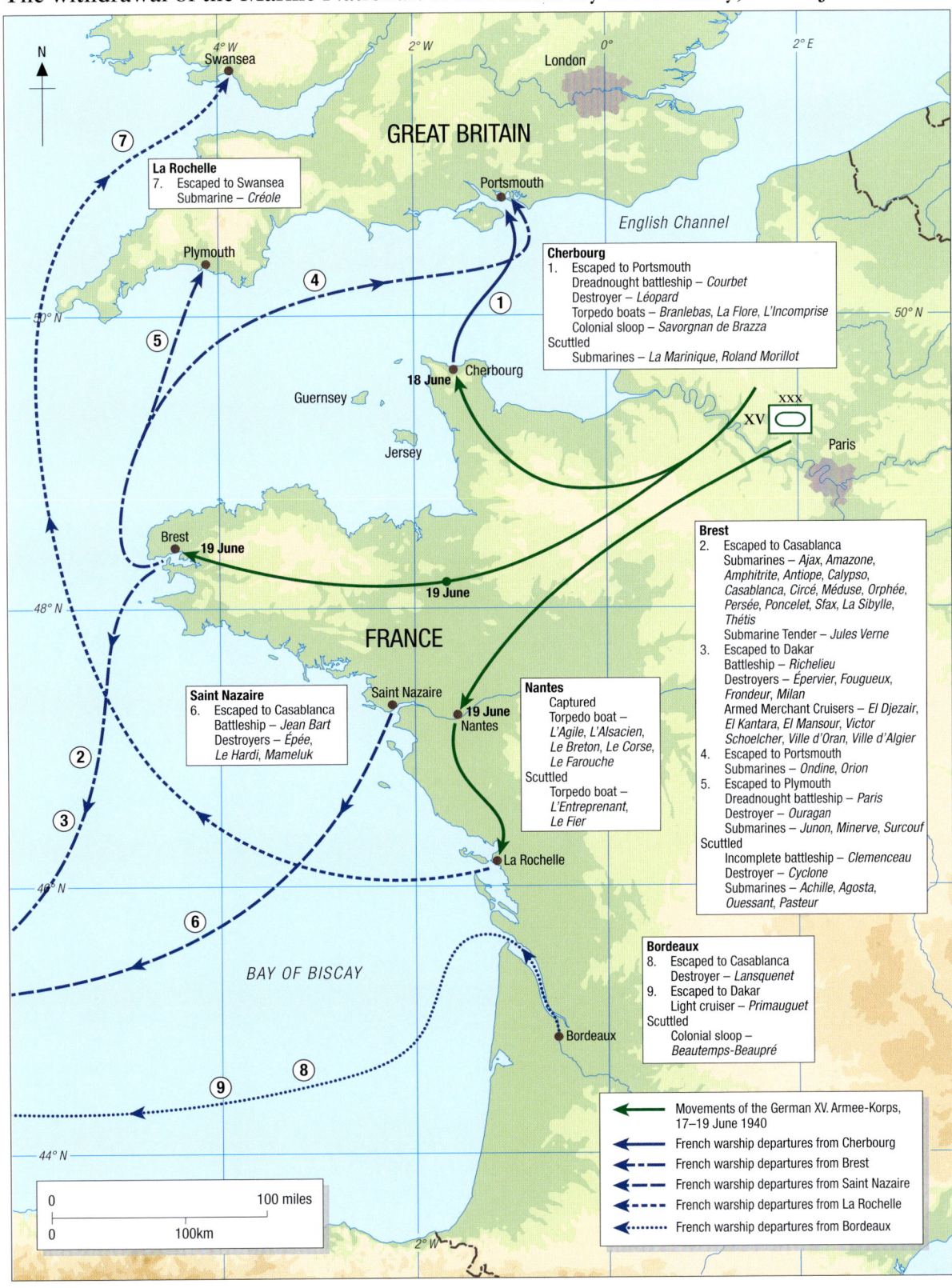

La Rochelle
7. Escaped to Swansea
   Submarine – *Créole*

Cherbourg
1. Escaped to Portsmouth
   Dreadnought battleship – *Courbet*
   Destroyer – *Léopard*
   Torpedo boats – *Branlebas, La Flore, L'Incomprise*
   Colonial sloop – *Savorgnan de Brazza*
   Scuttled
   Submarines – *La Marinique, Roland Morillot*

Brest
2. Escaped to Casablanca
   Submarines – *Ajax, Amazone,*
   Amphitrite, Antiope, Calypso,
   Casablanca, Circé, Méduse, Orphée,
   Persée, Poncelet, Sfax, La Sibylle,
   Thétis
   Submarine Tender – *Jules Verne*
3. Escaped to Dakar
   Battleship – *Richelieu*
   Destroyers – *Épervier, Fougueux,*
   Frondeur, Milan
   Armed Merchant Cruisers – *El Djezair,*
   El Kantara, El Mansour, Victor
   Schoelcher, Ville d'Oran, Ville d'Algier
4. Escaped to Portsmouth
   Submarines – *Ondine, Orion*
5. Escaped to Plymouth
   Dreadnought battleship – *Paris*
   Destroyer – *Ouragan*
   Submarines – *Junon, Minerve, Surcouf*
   Scuttled
   Incomplete battleship – *Clemenceau*
   Destroyer – *Cyclone*
   Submarines – *Achille, Agosta,*
   Ouessant, Pasteur

Saint Nazaire
6. Escaped to Casablanca
   Battleship – *Jean Bart*
   Destroyers – *Épée,*
   Le Hardi, Mameluk

Nantes
   Captured
   Torpedo boat –
   L'Agile, L'Alsacien,
   Le Breton, Le Corse,
   Le Farouche
   Scuttled
   Torpedo boat –
   L'Entreprenant,
   Le Fier

Bordeaux
8. Escaped to Casablanca
   Destroyer – *Lansquenet*
9. Escaped to Dakar
   Light cruiser – *Primauguet*
   Scuttled
   Colonial sloop –
   Beautemps-Beaupré

Movements of the German XV. Armee-Korps,
17–19 June 1940
French warship departures from Cherbourg
French warship departures from Brest
French warship departures from Saint Nazaire
French warship departures from La Rochelle
French warship departures from Bordeaux

Konteradmiral Lothar von Arnauld de la Perière (standing in boat, second from left) and Generalfeldmarschall Walter von Reichenau (standing in boat, third from left) touring the captured arsenal de Brest. When the naval base surrendered on the evening of 19 June 1940, all of the significant vessels of the Marine Nationale had evacuated or had been scuttled. (Image Bank WW2 – NIOD)

for compassion and consideration for the other side. Anxieties and suspicions would be further exacerbated in the coming days due to the ongoing breakdown of French communications networks as the Germans continued their advance. Messages between London and the new government at Bordeaux now took hours, and in some cases over 20 hours, to be received. The increasing lack of communication from Pétain's government during the days of armistice negotiations only fed the fires of speculation which were already raging in Churchill's mind and would lead to increasingly desperate courses of action.

Anticipating a negative British reaction to ordering Marine Nationale vessels to North Africa, at Darlan's prompting, Pétain's government made a unanimous declaration on 18 June that its fleet would be definitively kept out of Axis hands and that any armistice proposal which called for the fleet's surrender would be rejected out of hand. This was of some comfort to the British Admiralty, but what more significantly spoke to its concerns was the mass exodus of French naval units from Normandy and Brittany beginning on 17 June. Both Pétain and Darlan would be found true to their word regarding the evacuation of French vessels from and the destruction of facilities in ports threatened by German capture in the coming days. Due to Darlan's proactive efforts, the vast majority of vessels of the Marine Nationale had successfully escaped from Metropolitan France by the end of 19 June and were prepared to continue the war from bases outside of the Continent. On the following day in the Mediterranean, Amiral Godfroy demonstrated that the Marine Nationale was still in the fight. The cruisers *Suffren* and *Duguay-Trouin*, joined by three Royal Navy destroyers, conducted a sweep of the waters off Tobruk in Italian Libya while the battleship *Lorraine* left Alexandria the same day with the Royal Navy's light cruisers *Neptune*, *Orion*, and *Sydney*, and four destroyers for a bombardment of Bardia, on the Egyptian–Libyan border, early the following morning. Thus, on 21 June, as French negotiators travelled to the Forest of Compiègne to discuss armistice terms with their German counterparts, the Marine Nationale was still on the offensive in the Mediterranean.

All of these actions had improved Darlan's standing within the British Admiralty, as had a meeting between Darlan and First Lord of the Admiralty Albert Alexander and First Sea Lord Sir Dudley Pound in Bordeaux on 18 June. Darlan again stated that the French fleet would never fall into Axis hands while under his command, and he updated his British colleagues on the ongoing French naval offensive operations in the Mediterranean. He also explained how he had redirected available French merchant shipping to the Mediterranean in the event the French government decided to continue the war from North Africa and a mass military evacuation was ordered. The French merchant marine was already actively assisting the Armée de l'Air (French Air Force) with its mass redeployment to North Africa, shipping ground crews, ammunition, and other logistical necessities. This brief optimistic uptick was strengthened on 20 June when Lord George Lloyd, Secretary of State for the Colonies, reported to the War Cabinet on a coded message, shared with him by Darlan, which the admiral had just sent to his senior commanders:

> The Admiral of the Fleet believes that he will be able to retain the command of the naval forces, and he is making the necessary arrangements for this.
>
> Should the Admiral of the Fleet be unable to exercise this command without restraint, the naval forces will come under the orders of Amiral de Laborde (Ouest), alternatively Amiral Estéva (Sud) and Amiral Abrial (Nord), or lastly under Amiral Gensoul (Atlantique – Force de Raid).
>
> All these Flag Officers or those who might be called upon to succeed them are to conform to the following general orders:
>
> To fight vigorously to the end as long as a regular French Government – independent of the enemy – has issued no orders to the contrary;
>
> To disobey all other governments;
>
> Whatever orders are received, do not let the enemy take possession of any intact warships.
>
> XAVIER 377

'XAVIER 377' was a coded signature that Darlan had previously shared with his commanders in order to authenticate that such priority messages were indeed from the admiral. In this message, Darlan not only outlined the succession of power within the Marine Nationale should something happen to him, but again reiterated his personal order to keep French vessels out of the hands of the Axis, regardless of any government decisions to the contrary. The continued French naval action in the Mediterranean and Darlan's independent initiatives seemed to suggest to the Admiralty that Darlan or his admirals might be compelled to fight on, particularly if the Axis demanded the surrender of the French fleet as one of the conditions for an armistice. Such was not to be the case, however.

On the afternoon of 21 June, Adolf Hitler stepped out of the infamous railway carriage in Compiègne where the terms of the 11 November 1918 Armistice had been dictated to the Germans 21 years before. He abruptly left the armistice negotiations, just beginning inside the carriage, in a premeditated gesture of disdain for his French opponents. As he was walking away from the carriage, *der Führer* was likely reflecting on the strategic gamble he was making at that moment. While the selection of the 1918 Armistice carriage as the site for the negotiations and his early departure from the meeting were intended to humiliate the French, the armistice terms that the French negotiators were being handed were not. As Général d'armée Charles Huntziger, head of the French armistice team, read the terms presented to him, he was somewhat shocked. Only the north-western part of France was to be occupied by the Germans, and only until a final peace treaty was signed. There was no demand for French colonial territory. Furthermore, there was no demand for the surrender of the warships of the Marine Nationale.

Only the day before, Hitler had a heated argument with Großadmiral Erich Raeder, commander of the German Kriegsmarine, who expected the bulk of the French fleet to be surrendered into German hands. Just weeks before, Raeder's fleet had lost a heavy cruiser, two light cruisers, and ten destroyers during the Norway campaign while his only two battleships had both been damaged, reducing the Kriegsmarine's effective operational strength to a task force. Even though it would take months to raise and train crews to man them, as well

Adolf Hitler and Großadmiral Erich Raeder. In spite of Raeder's demands that French warships be handed over to the German Kriegsmarine as an armistice condition, Hitler insisted on lenient terms with regards to the Marine Nationale in an effort to more quickly bring about France's exit from the war. (Universal History Archive/Getty Images)

as considerable logistics efforts to outfit them, Raeder wanted modern vessels of the Marine Nationale incorporated into the Kriegsmarine to compensate for the losses off Norway and to create a better balance of power in the North Sea if an invasion of Great Britain was to prove necessary. He also asked for French territory in West Africa for the establishment of U-boat bases there in order to target British merchant shipping in the Central and South Atlantic. Raeder was thinking strategically in terms of a protracted war with the British.

Hitler completely disagreed with Raeder, however, and denied the admiral the opportunity of seizing French warships. The reason for such relatively lenient terms from such a vindictive potentate: Hitler wanted France out of the war as quickly as possible. He did not wish to expend further military resources occupying the whole of France, and the German armed forces were not in a position to effectively prosecute the war in North Africa if the French decided to fall back across the Mediterranean. Hitler's attention was now focused on bringing the British rapidly out of the war, either through negotiation or subjugation. Indeed, the very reason why he did not demand the surrender of the French fleet was that he did not want to run the risk of its vessels joining the already formidable strength of the Royal Navy. If invasion of the British Isles proved to be necessary to take the British out of the conflict, Hitler believed that the Luftwaffe could provide proper protection for amphibious assault vessels in the English Channel. At the time, Hitler was gambling on a negotiated peace or a quick knockout blow to take Great Britain out of the war; he did not want to have to turn to a lengthy naval blockade campaign that would require extensive German naval assets.

Article VIII of the Armistice of Rethondes, dealing with the status of the Marine Nationale, read as follows:

> The French war fleet is to collect in ports to be designated more particularly, and under German and/or Italian control to demobilize and lay up – with the exception of those units released to the French Government for protection of French interests in its colonial empire.
>
> The peacetime stations of ships should control the designation of ports.
>
> The German Government solemnly declares to the French Government that it does not intend to use the French War Fleet which is in harbours under German control for its purposes in war, with the exception of units necessary for the purposes of guarding the coast and sweeping mines.
>
> It further solemnly and expressly declares that it does not intend to bring up any demands respecting the French War Fleet at the conclusion of a peace.
>
> All warships outside France are to be recalled to France with the exception of that portion of the French War Fleet which shall be designated to represent French interests in the colonial empire.

When these terms were passed along to the French government, Pétain and Darlan instructed their representatives to request an alteration to Article VIII: that vessels of the Marine Nationale not required for colonial defensive purposes be berthed in North African ports with half their complements, after being demobilized and disarmed under Axis supervision. Darlan hoped to keep his vessels out of occupied German territory, where many of his warships' peacetime stations were located. He told the representatives that the threat of British air attack upon the ports in occupied France would be a significant threat to French warships demobilized there. Generaloberst Wilhelm Keitel, the head of the German armistice negotiators, dismissed this request, imperiously stating that the French were neglecting the generosity of the overall terms by arguing minor points, and insisted that the armistice terms be unaltered. Keitel then stated that the berthing locations of warships could be negotiated after the armistice was signed. He pointed to the particular wording of the appropriate clause in Article VIII, emphasizing the use of the word *soll*, or 'should': *Maßgebend für die Bestimmung der Häfen soll der Friedensstandort der Schiffe sein* (The peacetime stations of ships *should* control the designation of ports). Thus, Keitel inferred that the French could make an argument for the stationing of their warships in North Africa, an argument which would likely be heeded, under the indefinite language specifically used in this clause. Keitel's argument satisfied Pétain's government, given that the fleet was not to be surrendered and that the Germans appeared to be amenable to continued negotiations, and its negotiators signed the armistice at 1850hrs on 22 June 1940. It would officially go into effect six hours after a subsequent armistice was signed between France and Italy, which would be concluded two days later on the evening of 24 June.

INCREASING MISTRUST AMONG FORMER ALLIES

Across the Channel in London, the War Cabinet received notification in the early morning hours of 22 June that the French government had received armistice terms the day before. Cabinet ministers spent most of the day waiting for the exact details of the terms due to the ongoing communication difficulties and delays with British diplomats in Bordeaux. By evening, the War Cabinet had finally received the armistice terms in their entirety, including a report on the French amendments to Article VIII, and met at 2130hrs to discuss them. Churchill, in particular, voiced his dissatisfaction regarding the naval clauses and stated that German promises were not worth the paper they were written on. He then added:

> In a matter so vital to the safety of the whole British Empire we could not afford to rely on the word of Admiral Darlan. However good his intentions might be, he might be forced to resign and his place taken by another Minister who would not shrink from betraying us. The most important thing to do was to make certain of the two modern battleships *Richelieu* and *Jean Bart*. If these fell into the hands of the Germans, they would have a very formidable line of battle when *Bismarck* was commissioned next August. Against these fast and powerful ships we should have *Nelson*, *Rodney* and the older battleships like *Valliant*. *Strasbourg* and *Dunkirk* [sic] would certainly be a great nuisance if they fell into the hands of the enemy, but it was the two modern ships which might alter the whole course of the war … at all costs *Richelieu* and *Jean Bart*, particularly the former, must not be allowed to get loose.

After this belligerent statement, the War Cabinet received word that Pétain's government had signed the armistice several hours before. Again, Churchill was furious at what he considered to be French perfidy: that Pétain's government had not consulted the British prior to signing the armistice, and again invoking its failure to send French warships to British ports as a prerequisite to the armistice negotiations. Members of the War Cabinet convinced the flustered Prime Minister not to make any immediate military moves against French warships until final attempts had been made to persuade Darlan, or his admirals in North Africa, to rally with the British against Pétain's government or to scuttle their vessels. Time would also be needed for the Admiralty to make an effective appraisal of the now-altered naval situation in the Mediterranean and, if necessary, to develop plans to neutralize potential French targets with the limited resources at its disposal. The military option was heavily in Churchill's thoughts, however; Darlan could no longer be trusted as he was a minister within the government that agreed to the armistice.

The next several days saw numerous seemingly impulsive diplomatic efforts on the part of the British government and the Admiralty to undermine the armistice, which would go into effect on the morning of 25 June. First Lord of the Admiralty Alexander and First Sea Lord Pound sent messages to Darlan on the morning of 23 June, imploring him to continue to fight or send his vessels to British ports, reminding him of the armistice precondition which they still assumed had been communicated to Pétain's government. On the surface, Darlan politely responded with his, as usual by now, reply that he would never allow his ships to fall into Axis hands, but was confused and annoyed by the reference to a precondition he was hearing for the first time; he assumed it was some sort of duplicitous last-ditch strong-arming on the part of the British. Several other French admirals and colonial administrators were approached by British envoys beginning on 23 June, sounding out their thoughts on the armistice and the possibility of continuing the fight on the Allied side. The responses were almost uniform: while bitter about the terms of the armistice, with many still sympathetic to the British cause, no admiral in North Africa or colonial leader there would defy what they termed to be a legitimate French government. Most had faith in Pétain's efforts to preserve the French state and empire, while the admirals in particular were absolutely loyal to Darlan.

Perhaps the most pivotal meeting took place on the morning of 24 June when Vice Admiral North arrived at Oran from Gibraltar in an attempt to persuade Vice-Amiral Jean-Pierre Estéva, commandement des forces navales françaises du Sud, and one of Darlan's potential successors to command the Marine Nationale, to take control of Marine Nationale units in North Africa and to fight on alongside the Allies. Estéva was away that morning but North did meet with Vice-Amiral Marcel-Bruno Gensoul, commander of the Force de Raid. Gensoul was another of Darlan's 'heirs' and he was a known Anglophile who had successfully cooperated in several missions with the Royal Navy in the early months of the war. Gensoul, loyal to Darlan, however, was not to be persuaded either, stating

The incomplete French battleship *Jean Bart* moored at Casablanca following her escape from Saint Nazaire on 19 June 1940. Although she only had one operational primary turret and half of her powerplant, Churchill still viewed her as a significant potential threat to the Royal Navy. (Author's collection)

he would continue to obey the orders of a legitimate French government. While Gensoul was sympathetic to Britain's ongoing war, he personally believed that the British would not be able to withstand the German onslaught alone and that giving French warships to an ally which would likely soon be forced to the negotiating table seemed to be a fool's errand. As North departed for Gibraltar aboard a destroyer, he carefully followed another order he was given from the Admiralty: he observed and took careful notes about the defences around the naval base at Mers el-Kébir, to the west of Oran, as well as the mooring locations of Gensoul's warships there. North's report would be delivered to the War Cabinet that evening; with it, Churchill began contemplating the possibilities for an attack.

Other last-ditch diplomatic efforts over these days likewise did not bear fruit for the British, and three particular episodes involving Darlan caused the War Cabinet to increasingly doubt the admiral's credibility and allegiance. The first episode began on 21 June when 27 French parliamentarians who were opposed to the armistice, including former Prime Minister Édouard Daladier, declared their intention to travel to North Africa in order to set up a government-in-exile provided the armistice negotiations collapsed. Darlan made an ocean liner, *Massilia* of the Compagnie de Navigation Sud-Atlantique, available that day and the statesmen departed. When *Massilia* arrived in Casablanca on 24 June, the statesmen learned that the armistice had been signed and they were subsequently detained on the ship, on Darlan's orders. The parliamentarians had fallen into a trap; Pétain did not want them present when the vote to sign the armistice was made and Darlan gave his assistance.

Back in Metropolitan France, Pétain and Darlan branded the statesmen aboard *Massilia* as deserters and traitors, with some arrested later that summer and put on trial. Word had belatedly reached the War Cabinet that a group of French statesmen had left for North Africa, possibly intent on setting up a government-in-exile. On 26 June, General Lord Gort, former commander of the BEF, and Alfred Duff Cooper, Minister of Information, flew to Rabat in order to make contact with this group. Upon arrival, they were denied access to the statesmen on the direct orders of résident général de France au Maroc (French Governor of Morocco) Général d'armée Charles Noguès, who also curtly informed the British visitors that they were to leave the following day. When a report of this encounter reached London, the War Cabinet concluded that Darlan was firmly in step with Pétain and his other ministers, and that the admiral would oppose any attempts to coerce French overseas territories or vessels of the Marine Nationale from breaking with Pétain's government.

Two other episodes, both involving shipments of gold from the Banque de France, evacuated from Brest only days before, solidified the War Cabinet's anti-Allied

Amiral Jean Louis Xavier François Darlan, who became Chef d'état-major de la Marine (Chief of Staff of the French Navy) on 1 January 1937. (Bettmann/Getty Images)

Poster showing the liner SS *Massilia* of the Compagnie de Navigation Sud-Atlantique. The detention of the anti-armistice French parliamentarians aboard the liner upon its arrival in Casablanca on 24 June 1940 helped to turn the opinion of Churchill's War Cabinet against Pétain and Darlan. (Author's collection)

BRÉSIL · ARGENTINE · URUGUAY
PAR LES PAQUEBOTS DE LA Cᴵᴱ DE NAVIGATION
SUD · ATLANTIQUE

assessment of Darlan. On 22 June, Darlan dispatched the six vessels of the 1ère Division de croiseurs auxiliaires (1st Auxiliary Cruiser Division), then at Casablanca, to depart for Dakar instead of their original destination of Halifax in British Canada. Knowing the armistice was about to be signed, Darlan intended to keep the gold aboard those vessels in French hands and out of British banks in Canada. When the British government learned of this manoeuvre, it protested to Pétain's government, particularly regarding the gold reserves of Poland and Belgium, nations that were still at war with Germany, which were part of the shipment. Pétain's government refused to release any of the gold and Darlan even ordered the battleship *Richelieu* out from Dakar to escort the gold-bearing vessels – and to ward off any potential British interference. In another incident beginning on 22 June, Darlan ordered the light cruiser *Émile Bertin*, then at Halifax and also loaded with gold from the Banque de France, to proceed immediately to Martinique in the French West Indies. A day before, Darlan had given *Émile Bertin* the same order, but the cruiser's departure had been blocked by the Royal Navy and the Canadian authorities, stating that the gold would be safer in Canada. In the early morning hours of 22 June, *Émile Bertin* quietly slipped out of the Halifax harbour and headed south at maximum speed. She was shadowed by the British heavy cruiser *Devonshire* for part of her journey, and upon her arrival in Martinique on 25 June, *Émile Bertin* was greeted by the sight of the British light cruiser *Dunedin*, cruising off of Fort-de-France. *Dunedin*'s commander attempted to negotiate the return of the gold to Canada for safekeeping with the Marine Nationale commander for the Antilles, but this was also refused; the gold was offloaded and stored in vaults ashore, and the Haut Commissaire pour les territoires français d'outre-mer de l'Atlantique Ouest (High Commissioner for the French Overseas Territories of the Western Atlantic), Amiral Georges Robert, ordered *Dunedin* to leave several days later. On 28 June, the Admiralty learned of the reason for this rebuff from a deciphered message from Darlan to Robert at Martinique: it warned of the increasingly unfriendly attitudes of the British, instructed him to limit contacts with the Royal Navy, and to make safeguards against potential British offensive actions.

On the other side of the English Channel, Darlan had likewise become very wary of British intentions towards the authority of and decisions made by Pétain's government. This wariness began on the very first day of Pétain's rule, 17 June, when the Admiralty openly broadcast to all ships at sea instructions that forbade all Allied and neutral merchant ships from

Fast cargo vessel *Victor Schoelcher*, one of the fast transports of the 1ère Division de croiseurs auxiliaires (1st Auxiliary Cruiser Division) which transported gold from the Banque de France from Brest to Dakar. *Victor Schoelcher* carried the gold reserves of Poland and Belgium, the fate of which became a major issue of contention between the British government and Pétain's government. (Author's collection)

entering Metropolitan French ports. A subsequent message instructed merchant ships to ignore instructions from French broadcasting stations as they were now under German control. These orders came from Churchill who, without seeking War Cabinet approval, was keen to undermine the legitimacy of the new French rump state. Furthermore, in the days following the signing of the armistice, French warships and merchantmen in British ports were refused, under various pretences, from sailing for France. While the armistice negotiations were underway, Churchill worked hard to convince the War Cabinet to prevent any warships

French light cruiser *Émile Bertin* moored in the French Antilles following her escape from Halifax on 22 June 1940. (Author's collection)

or military cargoes from reaching France, where he postulated they would eventually end up in German hands. Darlan made multiple demands to the British government and Admiralty for the release of French warships and merchantmen in the coming days, but only merchantmen with foodstuffs and essential supplies were allowed to proceed to French Mediterranean ports. In Darlan's mind, the Royal Navy had, without directly saying so, instituted a blockade on the new French state.

Darlan was further angered by the British government's support of Général de brigade Charles de Gaulle, a junior member of Reynaud's government, who was laying the foundation of what was to become the Free France movement. Since 18 June, de Gaulle had been making broadcasts over the BBC, calling French servicemen to continue the fight against the Axis. After the signing of the armistice, de Gaulle began referring to himself as 'a member of the last independent French government' and openly criticized Maréchal Pétain, a revered figure in most French circles due to his successes in World War I. This infuriated the military and political authorities in Vichy France, including Darlan, particularly as de Gaulle was a relatively junior military figure and was a late addition to Reynaud's previous government. Several French leaders in Britain, as well as some British diplomatic personnel, complained to the British government that de Gaulle was an upstart and did not have the legitimacy, or following, to lead a successful French countermovement. In Churchill's mind, however, there was no one else stepping up to form a French resistance movement and, on 28 June, the War Cabinet – having been persuaded by Churchill – publicly announced, 'His Majesty's Government recognise Général de Gaulle as the Leader of all free Frenchmen, wherever they may be, who rally to him in support of the Allied cause.' These matters, combined with the British attempts to subvert the admirals under his command, rekindled the Anglophobia which had long been festering inside Darlan. On 27 June, he ordered that British vessels were to be turned away from French ports and denied supplies and fuel. On 1 July, during a meeting with the American ambassador to France, Darlan's attitude towards the post-armistice situation was made clear; he stated that Germany had clearly won the war and predicted, in a tone which hinted at gloating, that Great Britain would be overrun by Germany within five weeks and that the Royal Navy would prove as disappointing in combat as the French army had.

CHRONOLOGY

OPERATION *CATAPULT* (MERS EL-KÉBIR) AND OPERATION *LEVER*

1940

13 June	During *Fall Rot*, the renewed German offensive in Western Europe, the Wehrmacht breaches French defensive lines along the Rivers Seine and Marne. Paris falls the following day.
16 June	French président du Conseil des ministres Paul Reynaud, unable to persuade key military and political leaders to continue the war against the Axis, resigns, collapsing his government.
17 June	The new French government of retired maréchal de France Philippe Pétain requests armistice negotiations with the Axis powers.
17–19 June	Vessels of the Marine Nationale evacuate their bases in Normandy and Brittany prior to the arrival of German panzer columns and relocate to Mediterranean and African ports.
22 June	Pétain's government, without consulting the British government, signs the Armistice of Rethondes, formally taking France out of World War II.
23–26 June	At Prime Minister Winston Churchill's insistence, British politicians and Royal Navy officers attempt to persuade several French admirals to defy Pétain's government and sail their squadrons to British ports in order to continue the war against the Axis alongside the Royal Navy. These attempts fail.
24 June	On the orders of Amiral François Darlan, French colonial authorities in Casablanca detain a prominent group of anti-armistice French politicians who arrive aboard the liner SS *Massilia*.
25 June	The Marine Nationale begins demobilization in accordance with the terms of the Armistice of Rethondes.
27 June	Fearful of Axis designs on French warships, Churchill and the British War Cabinet decide to seek the transfer, surrender, or destruction of the Marine Nationale's Force de Raid in Mers el-Kébir, Force X at Alexandria, and the various French vessels in ports in Great Britain. Vice Admiral James Somerville is made commander of the Royal Navy's Force H at Gibraltar.
2 July	Admiral Somerville is given his final orders for Operation *Catapult*, in which he is to arrange the transfer, surrender, or destruction of the warships of the Force de Raid at Mers el-Kébir.

0558hrs, 3 July	Force H arrives off Mers el-Kébir. A negotiating party aboard the destroyer HMS *Foxhound* is sent into the harbour to confer with Vice-Amiral Marcel-Bruno Gensoul, commander of the Force de Raid.
0815–1725hrs, 3 July	Several rounds of failed negotiations take place between Somerville's representatives and Gensoul's representatives, and eventually Gensoul himself.
1215hrs, 3 July	After receiving a report of the situation at Mers el-Kébir from Gensoul, Darlan orders all Marine Nationale vessels in the western Mediterranean to sail to Gensoul's assistance.
1307hrs, 3 July	Somerville dispatches Swordfish torpedo bombers from the carrier HMS *Ark Royal* to mine the entrance to Mers el-Kébir harbour.
1725hrs, 3 July	Gensoul receives the following message from Somerville: 'If one of the British proposals is not accepted by 17:30 BST, I must sink your ships.' British negotiators leave Mers el-Kébir.
1754hrs, 3 July	Somerville gives the order to open fire.
1754–1804hrs, 3 July	HMS *Hood*, HMS *Valiant*, and HMS *Resolution* bombard Gensoul's battleships in Mers el-Kébir harbour. The battleships *Dunkerque* and *Provence* are damaged and eventually beach themselves, while *Bretagne* suffers several internal explosions and capsizes at 1809hrs.
1756–1803hrs, 3 July	Gensoul's destroyers *Volta*, *Le Terrible*, *Lynx*, and *Tigre* make their way out of Mers el-Kébir harbour, but *Mogador* abandons the escape after her stern is blown off by a British shell.
1756–1809hrs, 3 July	The battleship *Strasbourg*, her movements masked by smoke, manoeuvres into the harbour channel and escapes into the Bay of Oran.
1810hrs, 3 July	Gensoul orders his vessels to cease fire and requests Somerville do the same.
1831hrs, 3 July	Somerville learns of *Strasbourg*'s escape from Mers el-Kébir and orders his battleline to change course and pursue the French battleship.
1840hrs, 3 July	Six Swordfish from 818 Squadron, originally tasked with bombing Gensoul's remaining battleships in Mers el-Kébir, are instead ordered to attack *Strasbourg*.
1915–1940hrs, 3 July	Aéronavale flying boats attack Somerville's battleline. No hits are achieved.

1940hrs, 3 July	818 Squadron Swordfish attack *Strasbourg* but achieve no hits. Two torpedo bombers are lost to the battleship's anti-aircraft fire.
1950hrs, 3 July	The aircraft carrier HMS *Ark Royal* dispatches six torpedo-armed Swordfish from 820 Squadron to attack *Strasbourg*.
2020hrs, 3 July	With *Strasbourg* 40km ahead and with the sun setting, Somerville orders his battleline to give up the pursuit.
2050hrs, 3 July	820 Squadron Swordfish make torpedo runs against *Strasbourg* but all torpedoes miss.
3–4 July	Force H retires to a position 97km to the west-north-west of Oran as Somerville intends to launch an airstrike against Gensoul's remaining battleships on the morning of 4 July. Overnight, heavy fog sets in and Somerville abandons the follow-up mission at 0400hrs on 4 July.
4 July	Force H returns to Gibraltar at 1900hrs. *Strasbourg* and her destroyer escort arrive in Toulon at 2100hrs.
4–5 July	Darlan orders retaliatory airstrikes by Aéronavale bombers against Gibraltar. Two flights of five bombers make unsuccessful attacks during the late evening/early morning.
5 July	Somerville receives orders from the Admiralty to conduct another attack against the battleship *Dunkerque* in Mers el-Kébir on the morning of 6 July, codenamed Operation *Lever*. Force H leaves Gibraltar that evening.
0515–0620hrs, 6 July	Three waves of torpedo-armed Swordfish take off from *Ark Royal*.
0625hrs, 6 July	Six Swordfish from 820 Squadron attack *Dunkerque*. Five torpedoes miss and the sixth hits the patrol boat *Terre-Neuve*, moored alongside the battleship, but fails to explode.
0650hrs, 6 July	Three Swordfish from 810 Squadron make their torpedo runs against *Dunkerque*. One torpedo explodes against *Terre-Neuve*, splitting the patrol boat in two.
0655hrs, 6 July	14 depth charges aboard the wreck of *Terre-Neuve* explode, wrenching open *Dunkerque*'s starboard side and causing significant damage.
0700hrs, 6 July	Another three Swordfish from 810 Squadron attack *Dunkerque*. One torpedo strikes the harbour tug *Estérel*, sinking her.
1830hrs, 6 July	Force H returns to Gibraltar.
10 July	Darlan orders a retaliatory airstrike against Force H, detected at sea in the western Mediterranean. That afternoon, Armée de l'Air bombers fail to locate the British task force.

OPPOSING COMMANDERS

At this point it is necessary to discuss the reasons for the rigidity in strategic outlook of the two key players in this narrative, as well as introduce their subordinates who would be at the centre of the coming debacle at Mers el-Kébir – the opening battle in the last Anglo-French war.

BRITISH

Prime Minister Winston Churchill (1874–1965) and his grim determination to lead Great Britain through World War II to total victory need little introduction or explanation. What might seem striking, and warrants some explanation, however, is Churchill's seeming ruthlessness in his approach to Britain's former ally in the immediate aftermath of the Armistice of Rethondes, an attitude which is somewhat toned down in his later recounting of this episode in the war. To some extent Churchill may not have fully been able, or perhaps willing, to comprehend what he perceived as willing French readiness to exit the war so quickly. Churchill's opposition to the appeasement of Adolf Hitler and the Nazi regime is well known. In the early 1930s, Churchill voiced his desire for a strong, isolationist Britain, but also for a strong France, with its *Cordon Sanitaire* – a system of defensive alliances with Poland, Czechoslovakia, Romania, and Yugoslavia – which could maintain peace against potential German aggression on the Continent.

Churchill repeatedly argued for rearmament so that Great Britain could speak, and potentially act, assertively in the growing diplomatic crises in the latter half of the decade. At that time, Churchill abandoned his views on British isolation and advocated for an Anglo-French alliance and, following the German annexation of Austria in the spring of 1938, the creation of a 'Grand Alliance', led by Great Britain and France, with Yugoslavia, Czechoslovakia, Hungary, Bulgaria, Greece, and Turkey, which would stand opposed to fascist aggression. Thus, it can be argued that Churchill, as a long-standing supporter of a powerful France and advocate of Anglo-French military cooperation, expected a more determined resolve to fight from his French counterparts. In understanding Churchill's own mentality and resolve on the matter, it is important to note that on 28 May 1940, the Prime Minister only narrowly survived an attempt by a faction within his War Cabinet, led by Foreign Secretary Viscount Halifax and which supported peace negotiations with Germany, to collapse his government due to his steadfast resolution to continue the war to total victory. Nevertheless, Churchill had only been the official voice of the British government since 10 May 1940 – the day of the German invasion of the West. He had only been a Member of Parliament throughout most of the decade leading up to the war and only became part of government when he was made First Lord of the Admiralty in September 1939. Prime Ministers Stanley Baldwin and Neville Chamberlain were reluctant to have a 'radical' Churchill, who opposed their appeasement efforts, in their governments – and it was the work of these governments, largely responsible for the limited and insufficient rearmament programmes and isolationist foreign policy which negated early alliance efforts against Hitler, that contributed to the catastrophic situation in the West in the late spring of 1940.

In the years leading up to the war, Baldwin's and particularly Chamberlain's appeasement efforts had undermined proactive French diplomatic and military planning to contain Hitler, and also Mussolini. The French had sought to maintain a military alliance with Great Britain immediately after World War I, but post-war British governments had no desire to find their nation entangled in another Continental war. The French continued to rally for an alliance with Great Britain throughout the interwar years, but to no avail. As Hitler rapidly rearmed in the late 1930s, the French increasingly believed a future war against Germany could not be effectively fought without British assistance. While the British internally acknowledged that they too needed French assistance in such a conflict, the Baldwin and Chamberlain governments capitalized on increasing French anxiety of a war with Germany in order to leverage French acquiescence in their appeasement efforts with Hitler and Mussolini. The Anglo-French relationship was now an unequal one in which the French chafed at having to rely upon *La perfide Albion*; it was a forced relationship, full of suspicions and doubt. With their army having borne the full weight of the German army on the Western Front for over four years, and almost crumbling from within due to mutiny and exhaustion, French generals panicked at both the

November 1939 photograph of Prime Minister Neville Chamberlain's (first row, third from left) War Cabinet. Churchill (second row, fourth from left) was brought into this cabinet as First Lord of the Admiralty. When Churchill formed his own government on 10 May 1940, Foreign Secretary Viscount Halifax (first row, first from left), who favoured peace negotiations with Germany, led a failed effort within Churchill's first War Cabinet to have the Prime Minister removed from power in late May 1940. (Fox Photos/Getty Images)

prospect of appeasement to Germany and the possibility of losing the British as an ally in a future conflict with Germany. In their view, the British could not fully comprehend the national anxiety of having to defend a lengthy land boundary with Germany. There was long-standing resentment among many French politicians and military leaders of the British priority for imperial defence and seeming readiness to allow French blood and French soil to slow German military aggression. The appeasement efforts of the Baldwin and Chamberlain governments, and their seeming lack of military resolve, generated the spectre of potential British abandonment of the Continent for the defence of their empire in the minds of the French military and political leadership. Thus, while Churchill may have failed to understand or consider the demoralized French appreciation of the military situation in Western Europe, Churchill's bellicose rhetoric, so different from his predecessors, seemed like quixotic bravado to the French leadership at this eleventh hour.

While Churchill seemed to have no sympathy for the French plight in June 1940, the admiral Churchill selected to eventually confront the French during the Mers el-Kébir campaign did. On 27 June 1940, **Vice Admiral Sir James Somerville (1882–1949)** was appointed commander of Force H, the Royal Navy task force hastily assembled for potential offensive operations in the western Mediterranean following the French withdrawal from the conflict. Somerville joined the Royal Navy in 1897 as a midshipman, serving for a time in the Far East and later training in the new technology of wireless telegraphy. During World War I, Somerville served as fleet wireless officer for the Mediterranean Fleet during the Gallipoli campaign. After the war, Somerville rose through the ranks, retiring from the service in early 1939 after achieving the rank of Vice Admiral and having served as Commander-in-Chief, East Indies. Somerville was quickly recalled to active duty after the beginning of World War II and ably assisted Admiral Sir Bertram Ramsay during the Dunkirk evacuations. Somerville had a deep respect for the officers and men of the Marine Nationale and was more appreciative of France's dire situation in June 1940 than Churchill was. His personal correspondence tells of an officer who had no desire to act ruthlessly towards his French comrades-in-arms when eventually called to do so. While the Mers el-Kébir campaign was Somerville's first independent command during World War II – one which he felt was a failure – he would go on to successfully lead the Royal Navy's presence in the western Mediterranean during the intense Malta campaign and then work to rebuild the Royal Navy's presence in the Indian Ocean and Pacific as Commander-in-Chief, Eastern Fleet from 1942 to 1944.

FRENCH

To understand the rationale of **Amiral François Darlan** (1881–1942) during the hectic events of June and early July 1940, one needs to briefly examine how Anglo-French interwar relations and disagreements affected the morale and judgement of the leadership of the Marine Nationale in the midst of the French collapse – something arguably not fully appreciated or understood by Churchill at the time. The Marine Nationale had undergone some limited modernization during the interwar years but also had its strength and potential limited by British efforts to regulate the naval balance across Europe. Resentment of the British and the Royal Navy ran deep within much of the leadership of

The 330mm guns being mounted into turret no. 1 aboard the French battleship *Dunkerque*. She and *Strasbourg* were designed to counter the Deutschland-class 'pocket battleships' of the German Reichsmarine and the Italian Regia Marina's modernized dreadnoughts of the Conte di Cavour and Andrea Doria classes. The quadruple gun arrangement in the primary turrets was a weight-saving measure, compelled by the tonnage limitations dictated by the Washington Naval Treaty. (Author's collection)

the Marine Nationale by the spring of 1940. During World War I, the Marine Nationale lost 40 per cent of its vessels, and all capital ship construction had been halted during the war, with construction and funding priorities shifted to the army. Great Britain had been the primary architect of the 1922 Washington Naval Treaty, which dictated naval parity between the French Marine Nationale and the Italian Regia Marina – a forced parity with a power that had been viewed by many in French leadership as a junior, and somewhat unreliable, partner in the previous war.

Owing to its greater pre-war total tonnage, the Marine Nationale was left with a fleet of older vessels in desperate need of overhauls in the wake of the Washington Naval Treaty; new capital ship acquisitions were out of the question at the time due to the tonnage limits of the treaty, funding limitations, and the wartime moratorium on construction – circumstances which embittered many within the Marine Nationale's officer corps to post-war naval disarmament efforts. In the late 1920s, when Italy's *Il Duce*, Benito Mussolini, freely espoused his goal of an Italian *Mare Nostrum* dominated by a powerful fascist battle fleet, French attempts to address Italian belligerency and amend the balance of power in the Mediterranean were rebuffed by the British during the negotiations of the London Naval Treaty of 1930, in which the British sought to limit the number of heavy cruisers and submarines being constructed by the Mediterranean powers. The British government of the 1930s largely adopted an appeasement mentality towards Mussolini's Italy in an effort to keep peace in the Mediterranean – the primary trade and communications line to Britain's Far Eastern colonies – and keep Italy as a potential ally against a resurgent Germany; these considerations trumped the Marine Nationale's concerns over potential Italian naval belligerency.

The British action which caused the most discord for the Marine Nationale was the signing of the Anglo-German Naval Agreement in 1935, which eliminated the draconian naval limitations placed upon Germany by the Treaty of Versailles and allowed the German Kriegsmarine to build a battle fleet to a 35:100 ratio in strength compared to the Royal Navy. The French leadership had not been informed of this agreement by the British government and were infuriated with British presumption that they alone could undo elements of the Treaty of Versailles without consultation of their former allies.

This was the state of affairs when François Darlan was promoted to Chef d'état-major de la Marine on 1 January 1937. Graduating from the *École navale* (Naval Academy) in 1901, Darlan entered the Marine Nationale at a time that saw France decline as the world's second greatest naval power to a position behind Germany, the United States, and Japan. Darlan chafed at the parity with Italy, enforced by the Washington Naval Treaty – a bitterness particularly espoused by long-serving inter-war Ministre de la Marine (Minister of the Navy) Georges Leygues, who also happened to be Darlan's godfather and mentor. With Leygues' backing, Darlan was rapidly promoted and, as Leygues' Chef de Cabinet, served as the Marine Nationale's representative during the negotiations of the London Naval Treaty in 1930.

In the summer of 1935, Darlan supported and was inspired by the decision of his predecessor, Chef d'état-major de la Marine Vice-Amiral Georges Durand-Viel, to break with the tonnage limitations of the Washington Naval Treaty and to pursue the construction of the two new 35,000-ton battleships of the Richelieu class, following the Anglo-German Naval Agreement. Darlan approved of this initiative as it was recently learned that new German and Italian battleship classes being laid down, the Scharnhorst and Vittorio Veneto classes respectively, were well over the tonnage limits dictated by agreements both nations had signed. Unlike his predecessors, Darlan was a very assertive personality who had political connections that would allow him to influence not just French naval strategy but also French foreign policy.

The foremost of these politicians was Édouard Daladier, who became Ministre de la Défense nationale et de la Guerre (Minister of Defence and War) in June 1936, and then Prime Minister in April 1938. Daladier shared Darlan's trepidation of Italian ambition, particularly after witnessing the effects of Mussolini's substantive assistance to the Spanish Nationalists during the Spanish Civil War and the Italian de facto occupation of the Balearic Islands during the conflict. Italy's departure from the League of Nations in December 1937, followed three months later by Germany's occupation of Austria, solidified Daladier's concerns and he increasingly turned his ear to Darlan's call for new naval construction. In the spring of 1938, Darlan pushed for and received a new naval construction programme that included two new battleships (*Clemenceau* and *Gascogne*), the two aircraft carriers of the Joffre class, two light cruisers, two *contre-torpilleurs*, 18 light destroyers, and 18 submarines – the largest French naval expansion effort in a generation. Darlan calculated that these new vessels would be enough for the Marine Nationale to hold its own against both the Kriegsmarine and the Regia Marina in a future war – without the support of the Royal Navy as he did not believe that British support in such a war could be completely relied upon.

While Darlan resented the British for their efforts at appeasement and efforts to limit the strength of the Marine Nationale, he was enough of a pragmatist to realize that they would be a valuable ally in the event of war with Germany, Italy, or both, particularly in the short-term due to the time needed for French naval yards to complete planned vessels and those under construction. Following the Munich Agreement in the autumn of 1938, the British government finally showed interest in limited joint military planning between Great Britain and France in the event of further fascist aggression. Clever French diplomacy in December 1938 finally drove the British into full joint planning and alliance negotiations with the French; the French government let it be known to the British that it was seeking a permanent territorial and peace settlement with Germany, and the thought of having to potentially fight Germany, Italy, and possibly Japan on its own finally convinced the British that France was an essential ally. As joint naval planning finally began, Darlan immediately proposed an aggressive strategy in the Mediterranean against Italy, arguing for a joint Anglo-French offensive which with numerical superiority could quickly neutralize the Regia Marina and cut the sea lanes to Italy's overseas territories; such a pre-emptive move could prevent any Axis effort to contest control of the Mediterranean and limit the conflict to terrestrial fronts on the Continent. Darlan's proposal

Amiral Darlan (left) and First Sea Lord Sir Dudley Pound (right) in London, December 1939. The First Sea Lord came to share Churchill's suspicions about Darlan's integrity in the days following the Armistice of Rethondes. (Central Press/Hulton Archive/Getty Images)

was met with a stiff rejection, however. While willing to make naval plans for a war with Germany, the British government adamantly persisted with a policy of maintaining Italian neutrality, fearing that a war in the Mediterranean might close the Royal Navy's most accessible route to the Far East, and thus allow Japan to wreak havoc upon Britain's Asian territories. The British government even attempted to persuade France to offer some of its African territory in return for Italian neutrality in a war involving Germany and/or Japan. To Darlan, this rhetoric reinforced a long-simmering belief among many in French leadership that the British were all too willing to sacrifice the interests – and territory – of their allies to protect the hegemony of the British Empire. This acrimony would come to cloud Darlan's mind, and the minds of many in French civil and military leadership, in the dark days of June 1940.

Like Admiral Somerville, **Vice-Amiral Marcel-Bruno Gensoul** (1880–1973), the commander of the Force de Raid, would likewise be a reluctant participant in the coming Mers el-Kébir campaign. Gensoul entered the Marine Nationale in 1898 as a midshipman, spending his first years of service in the Far East. He was then transferred to the Mediterranean, specializing in torpedo combat. During the first years of World War I, Gensoul served as a lieutenant aboard the battleship *Republique* in the Mediterranean, and in 1917 was given command of the destroyer *Fanfare*. During the interwar years, he served in several command positions – including for a time the battleship *Bretagne* – and staff positions and rose steadily in rank, being promoted to Vice-Amiral in 1937. When World War II began, Gensoul was personally selected by Darlan to command the Force de Raid, a squadron formed from the Marine Nationale's most potent vessels – the new battleships *Dunkerque* and *Strasbourg*, the aircraft carrier *Béarn*, the three modern La Galissonnière-class light cruisers *Georges Leygues*, *Gloire*, and *Montcalm*, and the eight new destroyers of the Mogador and Le Fantasque classes.

Gensoul was known at the time as an admirer of the British Royal Navy, and his friendly relations with British officers surely helped to secure for him this prestigious command. The primary task of the Force de Raid was to assist the Royal Navy in protecting the vital Atlantic sea lanes from commerce-raiding German battleships and heavy cruisers – *Dunkerque* and *Strasbourg* were the only Allied battleships able at the time to counter the German Scharnhorst-class battleships. Gensoul's vessels participated in several 'killer group' missions against German commerce raiders and convoy escort missions from September 1939 to April 1940, when the Force de Raid was transferred to Mers el-Kébir in the Mediterranean due to increasing fears of Italian entry into the war. As mentioned previously, following the Armistice of Rethondes, Gensoul was sympathetic to the strategic position the Royal Navy was placed in, but like his commander, Darlan, his loyalty to the French state and defence of its – and his commander's – prerogative outweighed all other considerations. After the Mers el-Kébir campaign, Gensoul was made Inspecteur général des forces maritimes et Chef du Service central des œuvres de la Marine. He retired from the Marine Nationale in 1942, having never again held a sea command.

OPPOSING FORCES

BRITISH

With all diplomatic efforts at securing the French fleet seemingly frustrated and Darlan being reported as increasingly hostile to British efforts to continue the war, the War Cabinet met at noon on 27 June to discuss the forcible neutralization of the powerful elements of the Marine Nationale. The first decision to be made was which ships and forces to target. Despite Churchill's obsession of the potential threats posed by *Richelieu* and *Jean Bart*, planners in the Admiralty had recently determined that neither posed an immediate threat to Royal Navy operations in the Mediterranean or Atlantic. *Jean Bart* was still far from being completed, with only part of her propulsion plant installed and only one primary turret operational. While *Richelieu* was almost fully operational, intelligence noted that she had only been able to load a very small supply of 380mm ammunition before her escape from Brest; her 152mm guns posed no serious threat to British battleships or heavy cruisers if encountered. Furthermore, both vessels were being kept under surveillance by Royal Navy vessels patrolling off their respective bases.

The War Cabinet then turned to a report which it had been reviewing for the previous three days. At a meeting on 24 June, the War Cabinet requested an appreciation from the Admiralty of the most pressing threats potentially posed by French warships if they were to fall into Axis hands. First Lord of the Admiralty Alexander returned with the requested report at a subsequent War Cabinet meeting later that evening: the modern battleships *Dunkerque* and *Strasbourg* posed the greatest danger to the Royal Navy, particularly if they were employed by the Regia Marina in the Mediterranean, as they would supplement several modernized and new battleships about to come into Italian service. The naval staff report also commented, however, that it would be some time (worst-case scenario two to three months) before these vessels could be adequately manned, armed, and mobilized by Axis crews, provided they fell into Axis hands relatively undamaged. The primary vessels available for an immediate operation against *Dunkerque* and *Strasbourg* were battleships HMS *Hood* and HMS *Resolution*, and aircraft carrier HMS *Ark Royal*, operating out of Gibraltar. The staff report further stated that if an attack were to be made on the French battleships at their present mooring positions in Mers el-Kébir, aerial torpedoes could not be deployed due to the narrow confines of the naval base. A surprise early dawn bombardment, made from long range by the 381mm batteries of the British battleships

French battleship *Richelieu* photographed putting to sea from Brest on 18 June 1940, with the old armoured cruiser *Waldeck-Rousseau* in the foreground. As with her sister *Jean Bart*, Churchill wanted *Richelieu* neutralized in the wake of the French surrender, but analysts within the Admiralty did not deem it as an immediate threat to the Royal Navy as the French battleship had departed Brest with very little heavy-calibre ammunition. (Author's collection)

coupled with an aerial attack with conventional bombs, was thought to offer the greatest chance of success, but such a course of action could possibly lead to damage or destruction for one or both of the battleships employed, particularly if a Regia Marina task force appeared during the battle. In spite of the operational limitations and the suggested risks, the War Cabinet decided that a course of action, based on this Admiralty assessment, be prepared, to be executed on 3 July. In addition to the operation at Mers el-Kébir, the Admiralty also decided that the French vessels of Force X at Alexandria and French warships in ports in Great Britain were to be similarly secured or neutralized on the same day; Operation *Catapult* was born.

Already during the negotiations that culminated in the Armistice of Rethondes, Churchill began openly talking about the potential use of force against the most potent units of the Marine Nationale in a pre-emptive effort to keep them out of Axis hands. Such a task would have to fall to the Royal Navy, as the bulk of the Marine Nationale had relocated to the western Mediterranean and West Africa – regions where the British Army and RAF had little presence and were unable to effectively operate. For the Royal Navy, it was a difficult time to consider a new theatre of operations as its resources were already being greatly stretched by the German U-boat campaign and Italy's recent entry into the conflict. Nevertheless, even if military action against the French had not been contemplated, a Royal Navy force would still have to take over the defence of the western Mediterranean from Regia Marina incursions – a responsibility previously held by the Marine Nationale. This dilemma resulted in the creation of Force H. The Royal Navy had few ships in the western Mediterranean at that time and a majority of Force H's vessels were drawn from the Home Fleet – particularly a number of vessels that had just returned home from the abortive Norwegian campaign – as well as vessels that had been serving on convoy duties. On 18 June, the Admiralty dispatched the Admiral-class battlecruiser/fast battleship HMS *Hood* and the aircraft carrier HMS *Ark Royal*, accompanied by the F-class destroyers HMS *Faulknor* and HMS *Fearless*, from the Home Fleet, sending them to Gibraltar to form the nucleus of Force H. Several days later, the F-class destroyer HMS *Foxhound* was sent out from Britain and, on 26 June, the Queen Elizabeth-class modernized dreadnought battleship HMS *Valiant*, escorted by the E-class destroyer HMS *Escort* and the F-class destroyers HMS *Foresight* and HMS *Forester*, departed Scapa Flow for Gibraltar. The Revenge-class dreadnought battleship HMS *Resolution* arrived in Gibraltar on 28 June, detached from convoy duties, and on the following day, the Emerald-class light cruiser HMS *Enterprise* departed Plymouth with orders to join Force H. The Arethusa-class light cruiser HMS *Arethusa* and the destroyers of

13th Destroyer Flotilla, all based at Gibraltar, were also assigned to Force H; the A-class destroyer HMS *Active*, the Thornycroft type destroyer leader HMS *Keppel*, and the V/W-class destroyers HMS *Vidette*, HMS *Vortigern*, and HMS *Wrestler* from 13th Destroyer Flotilla would be tasked with participating in Operation *Catapult*. By 1 July, Force H was assembled.

While *Ark Royal* was the most capable aircraft carrier in active service with the Royal Navy at the time, her duties would be limited to aerial reconnaissance, gunnery spotting, aerial mine laying, and conventional aerial bombardment missions during Operation *Catapult* due to the narrow confines of the Mers el-Kébir harbour. Her presence was also necessary to counter any potential efforts by the Regia Marina to interfere in the operation. The effective neutralization of the French battleships would be undertaken by the BL 15in (381mm) Mark I guns aboard *Hood*, *Valiant*, and *Resolution*. An 879kg APC shell fired from one of these guns could penetrate 422mm of side armour plate at a distance of 9,144m or 297mm of armour plate at 18,288m. As *Dunkerque*'s armoured belt was only 225mm at its thickest and *Strasbourg*'s 283mm, and with both ships having only a maximum of 115–127mm thick deck armour, the British battleships' big guns were easily more than a match for the French fast battleships. The modernized dreadnought battleships *Bretagne* and *Provence* were also stationed at Mers el-Kébir, but their armoured belts only had a maximum thickness of 250mm and their deck armour was minimal. The armour protection for the primary turrets of the French fast battleships and modernized dreadnoughts ranged 250–360mm on the front and sides but this was also vulnerable to British 381mm fire. Based on these figures, it was calculated that the 381mm guns of *Hood*, *Valiant*, and *Resolution* could inflict critical damage on the French vessels from maximum visibility range. This distance would help somewhat to offset defensive fire from the French battleships' primary guns, as well as several heavier calibre coastal artillery batteries which were positioned around Mers el-Kébir. It was also calculated that the lighter guns aboard the light cruisers *Arethusa* and *Enterprise*, as well as those aboard the escorting destroyers, could assist in supressing the fire of the coastal batteries.

FRENCH

The deployment of the 24 381mm guns aboard *Hood*, *Valiant*, and *Resolution* was not a guarantee of success for Operation *Catapult*, however, as the capabilities of the French vessels in Mers el-Kébir could not be fully underestimated. While *Dunkerque* and *Strasbourg* had lighter armour protection than the other battleships (as their originally intended opponents were the lightly protected German Deutschland-class *Panzerschiffe*), the 330mm/50 Modèle 1931 guns of the French vessels had armour-piercing shells, which were developed to counter the stronger armour of the German Scharnhorst-class battleships. A French 570kg OPf Mle 1935 SAPC shell could penetrate 342mm of side armour at a distance of 23,000m, placing these guns among the best long-range naval artillery of the time. This capability posed a threat to Force H's World War I-era battleships, as *Hood*'s armoured belt was only 305mm at its thickest point, while both *Valiant*'s and *Resolution*'s were only 330mm. The older 340mm/45 Modèle 1912 guns aboard *Bretagne* and *Provence* were not as effective as the British 381mm guns or the modern 330mm

Disposition of the Marine Nationale, 3 July 1940

1. Algiers
   Light cruisers – *La Galissonnière, Georges Leygues, Gloire, Jean de Vienne, Marseillaise, Montcalm*
   Destroyers – *L'Audacieux, Le Fantasque, L'Indomptable, Le Malin, Simoun*
2. Alexandria
   Dreadnought battleship – *Lorraine*
   Heavy cruiser – *Suffren*
   Light cruisers – *Duguay-Trouin, Duquesne, Tourville*
   Destroyers – *Basque, Forbin, Le Fortuné*
   Submarine – *Protée*
3. Beirut
   Colonial sloop – *La Grandière*
   Submarines – *Achéron, Actéon, Dauphin, Espadon, Phoque*
4. Bizerte
   Destroyer – *L'Alcyon*
   Torpedo boats – *Bombarde, L'Iphigénie, La Pomone*
   Submarines – *Argo, Caïman, Fresnel, Henri Poincaré, La Sultane, La Vestale, Le Centaure, Le Tonnant, Monge, Pascal, Pégase, Saphir, Turquoise, Vengeur*
5. Bône
   Submarine – *Redoubtable*
6. Casablanca
   Battleship – *Jean Bart*
   Destroyers – *Épée, Fougueux, Frondeur, Le Hardi, Lansquenet, Mameluk*
   Colonial sloop – *D'Entrecasteaux*
   Submarines – *Ajax, Amazone, Amphitrite, Antiope, Bévéziers, Calypso, Casablanca, Circé, La Sibylle, Méduse, Orphée, Persée, Poncelet, Sfax, Sidi Ferruch, Thétis*
7. Dakar
   Battleship – *Richelieu*
   Light cruiser – *Primauguet*
   Destroyers – *Épervier, Fleuret, Milan*
   Colonial sloop – *D'Iberville*
   Submarines – *Le Glorieux, Le Héros*
8. Great Britain
   Dundee
   Submarine – *Rubis*
   Plymouth
   Dreadnought battleship – *Paris*
   Destroyers – *Mistral, Ouragan, Le Triomphant*
   Torpedo boat – *Bouclier*
   Submarines – *Junon, Minerve, Surcouf,*
   Portsmouth
   Dreadnought battleship – *Courbet*
   Destroyer – *Léopard*
   Torpedo boats – *Branlebas, La Cordelière, La Flore, L'Incomprise, La Melpomène*
   Colonial sloop – *Savorgnan de Brazza*
   Submarines – *Ondine, Orion*
   Swansea
   Submarine – *Créole*
9. Libreville
   Colonial sloop – *Bougainville*
10. Malta
    Submarine – *Narval*
11. Mers el-Kébir
    Battleships – *Dunkerque, Strasbourg*
    Dreadnought battleships – *Bretagne, Provence*
    Seaplane tender – *Commandant Teste*
    Destroyers – *Kersaint, Lynx, Mogador, Le Terrible, Tigre, Volta*

12. Oran
    Destroyers – *Bordelais, Boulonnais, Brestois, Casque, Le Corsaire, Tornade, Tramontane, Trombe, Typhon*
    Torpedo boat – *La Poursuivante*
    Colonial sloop – *Rigault de Genouilly*
    Submarines – *Ariane, Danaé, Diane, Eurydice, Oréade, Psyché*
13. Sfax
    Submarines – *Nautilus, Souffleur*
14. Sousse
    Submarines – *Marsouin, Requin*
15. Toulon
    Heavy cruisers – *Algérie, Colbert, Dupleix, Foch*
    Destroyers – *Aigle, Albatros, Cassard, Le Chevalier Paul, Le Flibustier, Gerfaut, Guépard, Lion, Le Mars, La Palme, Panthère, Tartu, Tempête, Valmy, Vauban, Vautour, Verdun*
    Torpedo boats – *Baliste, Bayonnaise*
    Submarines – *Archimède, Argonaute, Aréthuse, Atalante, Aurore, Cérès, Le Conquérant, Diamante, L'Espoir, Galatée, Iris, Naïade, Pallas, Perle, Sirène, Vénus*
16. Fort-de-France (Martinique, French Caribbean)
    Light cruiser – *Émile Bertin*
17. Pointe-à-Pitre (Guadeloupe, French Caribbean)
    Aircraft carrier – *Béarn*
    Light cruiser – *Jeanne d'Arc*
18. Saigon (French Indochina)
    Light cruiser – *Lamotte-Picquet*
    Colonial sloops – *Amiral Charner, Dumont d'Urville*

Disposition of the Marine Nationale, 3 July 1940

0 — 500 miles
0 — 500km

guns mounted on *Dunkerque* or *Strasbourg*, but they could not be ignored. Their 635kg armour-piercing shells could still penetrate roughly 320mm of side armour plate at a distance of 9,144m, making them a potent threat if the battle distance closed to a shorter range. Another particular advantage *Dunkerque* and *Strasbourg* held over their opponents was superior speed; both battleships could make a maximum speed of 29.5 knots. *Resolution* and *Valiant* could only make 22 and 23 knots, respectively, while *Hood* had a designed speed of 31 knots. After being in almost continuous service for 20 years and in dire need of a lengthy overhaul and modernization – both cancelled due to the outbreak of World War II – *Hood* was past her prime by the summer of 1940. She could only achieve a consistent maximum speed of 26.5 knots by this time, and if *Dunkerque* and *Strasbourg* were able to put out to sea at Mers el-Kébir, they could outrun all of Force H's battleships. A breakout attempt would further favour the French as the modern Mogador-class, Le Fantasque-class, and Chacal-class destroyers at Mers el-Kébir were all faster and had heavier firepower than Force H's destroyers. Furthermore, there was a sizeable force of French destroyers and a division of submarines stationed in nearby Oran, which could also be called upon to assist in a French breakout from Mers el-Kébir. Given these French capabilities, Force H's best chances of success laid in a quick and accurate heavy bombardment and taking all measures necessary to avoid a French escape to the sea.

ORDERS OF BATTLE

BRITISH

ROYAL NAVY

Force H, based at Gibraltar – Vice Admiral Sir James Somerville
Battleships HMS *Hood*, HMS *Resolution*, and HMS *Valiant*
Aircraft carrier HMS *Ark Royal*
Light cruisers HMS *Arethusa*, HMS *Enterprise*
8th Destroyer Flotilla – destroyers HMS *Escort*, HMS *Faulknor*, HMS *Fearless*, HMS *Foresight*, HMS *Forester*, and HMS *Foxhound*
13th Destroyer Flotilla – destroyers HMS *Active*, HMS *Keppel*, HMS *Vidette*, HMS *Vortigern*, and HMS *Wrestler*
Fleet Air Arm (embarked on *Ark Royal*) – Vice Admiral Lionel Wells
800 Naval Air Squadron (12x Blackburn Skua)
803 Naval Air Squadron (12x Blackburn Skua)
810 Naval Air Squadron (12x Fairey Swordfish)
818 Naval Air Squadron (9x Fairey Swordfish)
820 Naval Air Squadron (9x Fairey Swordfish)
1st Submarine Flotilla, based at Alexandria
Submarines *Pandora* and *Proteus*

ROYAL AIR FORCE

202 Squadron RAF, based at Gibraltar (Saunders Roe A.27 London Mk.II)

FRENCH

MARINE NATIONALE

Force de Raid, based at Mers el-Kébir – Vice-Amiral Marcel-Bruno Gensoul
1ère Division de ligne – battleships *Dunkerque* and *Strasbourg*
2ème Division de ligne – battleships *Bretagne* and *Provence*
4ème Division de contre-torpilleurs – destroyers *Lynx* and *Tigre*
6ème Division de contre-torpilleurs – destroyers *Mogador* and *Volta*
Other – destroyer *Le Terrible*
Marine Oran, based at Mers el-Kébir
Unassigned – seaplane carrier *Commandant Teste*, destroyer *Kersaint*
Marine Oran, based in Oran – Contre-Amiral Marcel Louis Hippolyte Jarry
5ème Division de torpilleurs – destroyers *Boulonnais* and *Brestois*
7ème Division de torpilleurs – destroyers *Tornade*, *Tramontane*, and *Typhon*
8ème Division de torpilleurs – destroyers *Bordelais* and *Trombe*
13ème Division de torpilleurs – torpedo boat *La Poursuivante*
14ème Division de sous-marins – submarines *Ariane*, *Danaé*, *Diane*, and *Eurydice*
18ème Division de sous-marins – submarines *Oréade* and *La Psyché*
Other – destroyers *Casque* and *Le Corsaire*, colonial sloop *Rigault de Genouilly*
Aéronavale
Escadrille HS-1, based at Arzew (6x Loire 130)
Escadrille E-2, based at Arzew (2x Bréguet 521 Bizerte)

ARMÉE DE L'AIR

Forces aériennes et des forces anti-aériennes de l'Afrique du Nord (AFN) et de la 5ème région aérienne – Général Roger Pennès
Groupe de Chasse I/5 based at Saint-Denis-du-Sig (35x Curtiss H-75)
Groupe de Chasse II/5 based at Saint-Denis-du-Sig (43x Curtiss H-75)
Groupe de Chasse II/3 based at Relizane (39x Dewoitine D.520 and 14x Morane-Saulnier M.S.406)
Groupe de Chasse III/3 based at Relizane (38x Dewoitine D.520 and 19x Morane-Saulnier M.S.406)
Groupe de Bombardement I/11 based at Blida (Lioré et Olivier LeO 451)
Groupe de Bombardement II/11 based at Blida (Lioré et Olivier LeO 451)
(Note – few of these aircraft were operational at the beginning of 3 July 1940)

OPPOSING PLANS

BRITISH

On the afternoon of 27 June, Vice Admiral Sir James Somerville stepped into the office of the First Lord of the Admiralty, having been immediately summoned. In this abrupt meeting, First Lord of the Admiralty Alexander informed Somerville that he was to take command of a task force, Force H, being assembled in Gibraltar and that his mission was to ensure the transfer, surrender, demobilization, or destruction of French warships presently stationed at Mers el-Kébir. Force H was to be an independent force, directly under the command of the Admiralty, and Somerville was instructed that he was to strictly follow the orders issued to him by the First Sea Lord; he would have little command discretion. This was a deliberate command arrangement given the relatively controversial mission he was about to undertake. Furthermore, Somerville's selection to lead this command, which passed over several senior officers, was heavily influenced by Churchill, who had been impressed with the admiral's previous assignment: organizing the Dunkirk evacuation under Vice Admiral Bertram Ramsay.

Finally, Somerville was told by First Lord Alexander that French morale had crumbled in recent days and that it was highly unlikely that the vessels at Mers el-Kébir would resist with force. Hesitant of this grave mission, but somewhat reassured by Alexander's assessment of French morale, Somerville departed for Gibraltar aboard light cruiser *Aurora* on the afternoon of 28 June. While Somerville was en route, the Admiralty informed its senior commanders that the purpose of Force H was to prevent vessels of the Regia Marina from breaking out of the Mediterranean and to conduct independent action against Regia Marina sorties and Italian coastal targets; this cover story was intended to keep the Mers el-Kébir operation a secret.

On 30 June, Admiral Somerville arrived in Gibraltar and reviewed his command. He then called together a meeting of his senior officers, as well as Vice Admiral North, who had conducted the failed meeting with Amiral Gensoul six days prior. When Somerville revealed Force H's actual mission, North and several other officers who had been part of the various diplomatic missions to the Marine Nationale were shocked at the heavy-handed approach decided upon by the War Cabinet and the Admiralty. They stated that they had observed that morale was still relatively high among Gensoul's crews and that the French admiral would likely put up stiff resistance if force was used. North stated that he was opposed to the use of force, believing

it could rapidly turn a defeated ally into a belligerent enemy, and did not understand the reasoning in London.

Somerville too began to wonder; why was the version of events from the men on the scene so different from that in which he had been briefed? After pondering this, Somerville sent a message to the Admiralty on the afternoon of 1 July in which he recommended abandoning the use of force to secure the vessels at Mers el-Kébir, based on the reports from Admiral North and his officers. Somerville included a caveat in his recommendation – 'Unless Their Lordships have more definite and contrary information I consider proposals merit very careful consideration…' – perhaps the Admiralty was aware of events that warranted heavy-handed action. Several hours later, a message came from the Admiralty stating that Somerville's recommendation was unacceptable and that if Gensoul did not accept British terms, then his ships must be destroyed. Admiral Cunningham, who had similarly been given orders to arrange the transfer, surrender, demobilization, or destruction of the vessels of French Force X in Alexandria harbour, had also protested against the use of force but was also told that his orders were to remain unchanged.

What Somerville and Cunningham were not privy to was Churchill's morbid fear of the French battleships falling into Axis hands and his rigid insistence on preventing that no matter what. The admirals were also not privy to pivotal information which had just come to the Prime Minister's attention. On 1 July, Churchill calculated that his window of opportunity for acting decisively against the French vessels might swiftly be closing. That day, the Admiralty received a decrypted message from the French *Amirauté* (Admiralty) to its liaison officer in London, stating that the Italian armistice commission had agreed to allow the warships of the Marine Nationale to be demilitarized in unoccupied ports in Metropolitan France and North Africa. It was believed that a similar concession would soon be granted by Germany. If this agreement was reached and French warships

Vice Admiral Sir Andrew Cunningham, commander of the Royal Navy's Mediterranean Fleet, who, like Admiral Somerville, was opposed to Churchill's insistence on belligerent action against Marine Nationale units. (Elliott & Fry/Hulton Archive/ Getty Images)

remained in French hands, he calculated that there would be little incentive for French naval officers to disobey their government and side with the British.

Furthermore, *Dunkerque*, *Strasbourg*, *Richelieu*, and *Jean Bart* would likely be transferred back to the major fleet base at Toulon, where the latter two could be made fully armed and operational. Toulon's defences were much more formidable than the vessels' present locations if they had to be subsequently attacked, but also the naval base was within easy reach of the German armed forces if Hitler decided to capture the vessels. Churchill also calculated that it would likely be more difficult to persuade the War Cabinet to attack the French vessels if it appeared that the Axis would actually allow the ships to remain out of the occupation zone. Churchill was aware of rumblings within service planning committees against offensive action; some officers believed that while several French vessels might be destroyed, such a drastic action might drive the French rump state and its empire into open warfare with the British, a move that would have severe strategic repercussions for the balance of the war. The majority opinion with regards to the French fleet within the service planning committees was for a patient, diplomatic approach. In Churchill's mind, however, German promises were worthless and all too many across Europe had fallen victim to them. At this time, the Prime Minister had the approval of the War Cabinet for offensive action against the French battleships and, with German preparations beginning for an invasion of Britain, the time to act was now and without question.

In the early morning hours of 2 July, Somerville received his operational orders for Operation *Catapult* from Churchill and the Admiralty:

His Majesty's Government have decided that the course to be adopted is as follows:

(a) French [Fleet] at [Oran] and Mers-el-kabir [*sic*] is to be given four alternatives –

　i.　To sail their ships to British harbours and to continue to fight with us.

　ii.　To sail their ships with reduced crews to a British port from which their crews would be repatriated whenever desired [or] in the case of alternative (i) or (ii) being adopted, the ships would be restored to France at the conclusion of the war or full compensation would be paid if they are damaged meanwhile…

　iii.　To sail their ships with reduced crews to some French port in [the] West Indies such as Martinique. After arrival at this [port] they would either be demilitarized, to our satisfaction, if so desired, or be entrusted to the USA jurisdiction for the duration of the war. The crews would be repatriated.

　iv.　To sink repetition sink their ships.

(b) Should [the] French Admiral refuse to accept all above alternatives and should he suggest he should demilitarize his ships to our satisfaction at their present berths, you are authorized to accept this further alternative provide[d] you are satisfied that measures taken for demilitarization can be carried out under your supervision with[in] six hours and prevent ships being brought into [service] for at least one year, even at a fully [equipped] dockyard port.

(c) If none of these alternatives are accepted by the French you are to endeavour to destroy repetition destroy ships in Mers-el-kabir [sic] [particularly] *Dunkerque* and *Strasbourg* using all means at your disposal. Ships at Oran should also be destroyed if this will not repetition not entail any considerable loss of civilian life.

Later that morning, Somerville brought together his commanders and explained his plan for the operation, which was to commence the following day. Phase I of the plan was different scenarios regarding the successful negotiation of Gensoul's force joining the British, sailing to British ports or French Caribbean ports, or allowing British demolitions crews to demilitarize its vessels. The destroyers *Keppel* and *Wrestler* embarked demolition teams for just this purpose. Phase II outlined the use of force should Gensoul reject the prior proposals. The first part of Phase II called for several rounds to be fired near the French battleships in order to compel their crews to abandon their vessels. Demolition parties would then be dispatched via *Keppel* and *Wrestler* to the harbour to destroy the abandoned warships. If organized resistance was encountered, Somerville's battleships were to destroy by long-range naval gunfire the targets in the following order: first *Dunkerque* and *Strasbourg*, second *Bretagne* and *Provence*, and lastly any other warships, in order of size, in Mers el-Kébir harbour. Torpedo bombers from *Ark Royal* would be dispatched to attack the French vessels with conventional bombs. Somerville's battleships would fire from a distance of roughly 16.5km in order to protect them from defence fire from the shore batteries around the harbour and to allow for plunging fire that would not only clear the 10m-high

'The Mighty *Hood*', Admiral Somerville's flagship during Operations *Catapult* and *Lever*. *Hood*'s eight 381mm guns and fast maximum speed were determined as critical in a potential combat action against the Marine Nationale's fast battleships *Dunkerque* and *Strasbourg*. (Author's collection)

Coastal defenses and Armée de l'Air and Aéronavale bases around Mers el-Kébir and Oran

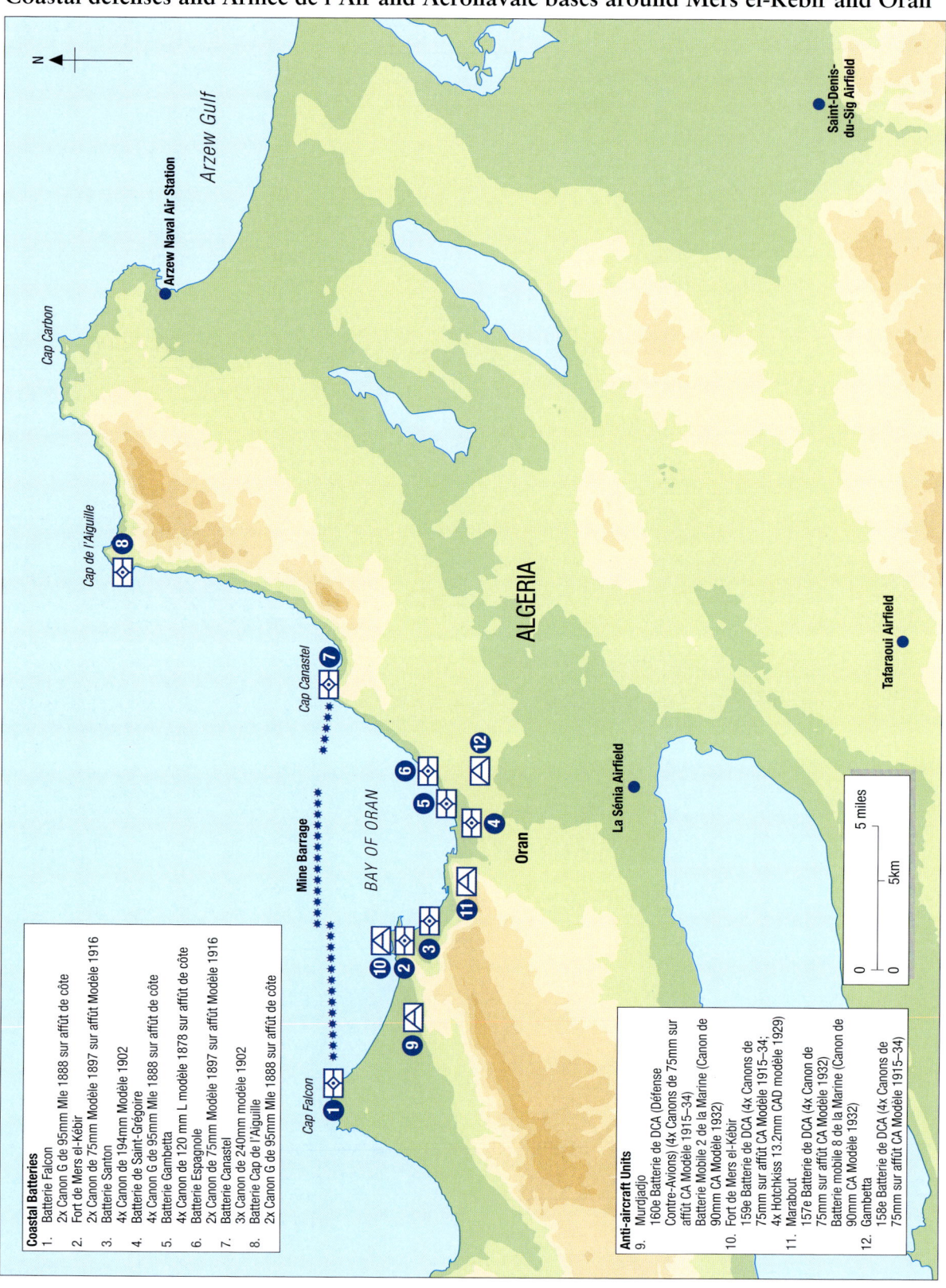

Arzew Gulf

Cap Carbon

Cap de l'Aiguille

Arzew Naval Air Station

Saint-Denis-du-Sig Airfield

ALGERIA

Cap Canastel

Tafaraoui Airfield

Mine Barrage

BAY OF ORAN

La Sénia Airfield

Oran

Cap Falcon

5 miles

5km

Coastal Batteries
1. Batterie Falcon
   2x Canon G de 95mm Mle 1888 sur affût de côte
2. Fort de Mers el-Kébir
   2x Canon de 75mm Modèle 1897 sur affût Modèle 1916
3. Batterie Santon
4. 4x Canon de 194mm Modèle 1902
5. Batterie de Saint-Grégoire
   4x Canon G de 95mm Mle 1888 sur affût de côte
6. Batterie Gambetta
   4x Canon de 120 mm L modèle 1878 sur affût de côte
7. Batterie Espagnole
   2x Canon de 75mm Modèle 1897 sur affût Modèle 1916
8. Batterie Canastel
   3x Canon de 240mm modèle 1902
   Batterie Cap de l'Aiguille
   2x Canon G de 95mm Mle 1888 sur affût de côte

Anti-aircraft Units
9. Murdjadjo
   160e Batterie de DCA (Défense Contre-Avions) (4x Canons de 75mm sur affût CA Modèle 1915–34)
   Batterie Mobile 2 de la Marine (Canon de 90mm CA Modèle 1932)
10. Fort de Mers el-Kébir
    159e Batterie de DCA (4x Canons de 75mm sur affût CA Modèle 1915–34;
    4x Hotchkiss 13.2mm CAD modèle 1929)
11. Marabout
    157e Batterie de DCA (4x Canon de 75mm sur affût CA Modèle 1932)
    Batterie mobile 8 de la Marine (Canon de 90mm CA Modèle 1932)
12. Gambetta
    158e Batterie de DCA (4x Canons de 75mm sur affût CA Modèle 1915–34)

concrete breakwater/quay to which the French battleships were moored but also allow shells to penetrate their thinner deck armour and explode deep inside. If the French ceased fire during the bombardment, demolition teams would then be sent in. With plans set, Force H raised anchor that afternoon, clearing Gibraltar's harbour at 1700hrs, and headed eastward. In the early morning hours of 3 July, Somerville received a final instruction from the Admiralty: regardless of whatever course of action Gensoul chose to take, the overall operation was to be completed before the sun set; the fuse had now been lit.

FRENCH

The situation at Mers el-Kébir on 2 July suggested anything but readiness for combat. The coastal batteries surrounding the harbour were in the process of demobilization and most of the guns had their breech blocks removed, in accordance with the terms of the Armistice of Rethondes. Reconnaissance flights by flying boats of the Force maritime de l'aéronautique navale (naval air force), or Aéronavale, from the base at Arzew had been curtailed due to a prohibition of French military flights. Aboard the warships in the harbour, the initial shock of the French surrender was beginning to subside among the crews, and the realities of the armistice conditions were beginning to set in. Eager to maintain whatever morale they could, officers had re-established peacetime regimes aboard ship, with an emphasis on recreational activities. Work was composed of routine duties and the beginning of disarmament projects as required by the armistice terms. What was in the immediate thoughts of most of the sailors, however, was the conditions of their families back in France and where their vessels would eventually be stationed; the final demobilization locations for Marine Nationale vessels were still being worked out by the armistice commission.

The vessels in Mers el-Kébir had not been rendered completely impotent yet, however. Amiral Gensoul clearly understood that he held the responsibility for the most potent operational vessels in the Marine Nationale. He had been privy to Darlan's recent messages about possible British hostile actions and took note of several reconnaissance flights over Mers el-Kébir made by British flying boats operating out of Gibraltar. With the aircraft of the Armée de l'Air grounded due to the terms of the armistice, Gensoul could only watch the aircraft slowly circle overhead and wonder what British intentions were. In order to respond to potential British hostile action, or perfidious Italian naval action against his ships – a more likely scenario to Gensoul at the time – all of his vessels were ordered to maintain a six-hour readiness and their fuel bunkers were kept full. In an attempt to compensate for demobilized coastal batteries, an aft 340mm turret aboard both *Bretagne* and *Provence* was kept manned and at the ready. Furthermore, all vessels kept their anti-aircraft crews on duty and their anti-aircraft batteries armed. At the harbour entrance, an armed trawler maintained patrol for submarines at the gate in the anti-submarine nets and a destroyer was kept at 90-minutes-readiness in the event of a submarine sighting. While these minimal preparations were technically in violation of the Armistice of Rethondes, Gensoul was reluctant to let his guard completely down as the war in the Mediterranean continued to rage.

OPPOSITE
The port of Mers el-Kébir was selected as a potential major fleet base by the Marine Nationale in 1934. Amiral Darlan began work on the fleet base in 1937 but only minimal defensive emplacements and facilities had been completed by the beginning of the war. Small piers were constructed at the western end of the harbour, near the village of Saint André, to accommodate two divisions of destroyers. For mooring larger vessels, a 1,000m concrete quay was built, extending to the south-east off the eastern tip of Fort de Mers el-Kébir. Off the coast, several minefields were laid from Cap Falcon to Cap Canastel across the Bay of Oran. Inside the harbour, a defensive boom of anti-submarine nets stretched eastward from the quay and then south to the Santa Cruz Fortress at the southern end of the bay, with a gate at the eastern end of the boom. The channel from the quay to the gate was very narrow due to shallow areas in the harbour, and limited the area of manoeuvre of larger vessels. Battleships had to be moored by the stern to the quay and then manoeuvred by tugs to make their way towards the harbour's exit, taking considerable effort and time. Being moored with their bows facing the south-west also placed battleships in a poor location for defensive fire; only aft turrets had a full field of fire facing the sea and the all-fore primary turrets of the Dunkerque-class battleships only had a limited radius of fire to starboard, with their limited field of fire partially obscured by Fort de Mers el-Kébir. Several shore batteries were completed by 1940 but their limited armament did not compensate for the battleships' inability to provide effective defensive fire. This map shows the locations of the coastal and anti-aircraft batteries located at Mers el-Kébir and around the Bay of Oran.

THE CAMPAIGN

FINAL NEGOTIATIONS

As dawn broke over the harbour of Mers el-Kébir on the morning of 3 July, the base's wireless station began to pick up signals from the British destroyer *Foxhound*. At 0558hrs, *Foxhound* requested permission to enter the harbour and later began signalling by light that Captain Holland of the Royal Navy wished to parley. Captain Cedric Holland, commander of *Ark Royal*, served as the British government's naval attaché in Paris for the first months of the war, and for this reason, as well as his cordial relations with much of the Marine Nationale's leadership, he was selected by Somerville to undertake the careful negotiations with Gensoul. At 0724hrs, *Foxhound* was granted access into the harbour, and she anchored outside the anti-submarine nets off the breakwater, not wanting to be trapped in the harbour if events were to take a dire course. At 0815hrs, Gensoul's aide-de-camp, Lieutenant de Vaisseau Bernard Dufay, arrived at *Foxhound*, bearing a message from the admiral: Gensoul was too busy to see Holland and the British were instructed to pass along any communications through Dufay. When Holland sent Dufay back with a message stating that he could only speak directly with Gensoul, *Foxhound* received a signal from Gensoul's flagship, *Dunkerque*, at 0845hrs: the destroyer was instructed to leave the harbour immediately. Intent on continuing negotiations, Holland and his aides boarded one of *Foxhound*'s boats and remained in the harbour while the destroyer sailed to a new position just offshore.

The capital ships of the Force de Raid at Mers el-Kébir, photographed from the seaplane tender *Commandant Teste* on her arrival in the harbour on 25 June 1940. From left to right are *Dunkerque*, *Provence*, *Strasbourg*, and *Bretagne*. (Collection Aubry Palouzier)

What Holland did not know was that Gensoul was already infuriated by the events of the morning without even having received the Royal Navy's ultimatum. While *Foxhound* was waiting to enter the harbour, she was signalling the following message in the direction of Gensoul's battleships: 'ADDRESSE A AMIRAL GENSOUL – The Royal Navy hopes that the proposals will allow you, the valiant and glorious Marine Nationale, to side with us. In this case your ships would always remain yours and no one would need any anxiety in the future. The British Fleet is off the coast of Oran to welcome you.' The intention of these signals was to make French crews aware of the negotiations underway, believing most junior officers were still willing to fight on in the event Gensoul tried to keep the proceedings to himself. Around 0840hrs, lookouts aboard *Dunkerque* spotted ships of a British task force on the horizon, confirming *Foxhound*'s signals that the Royal Navy was taking up position off Oran. A British Fairey Swordfish reconnaissance biplane, having taken off from *Ark Royal* at 0630hrs and flying over the Oran area, had also been reported. The threatening surprise appearance of a British task force offshore, the subversive signals from *Foxhound*, and the fact that a mere captain had been sent to conduct such a pivotal undertaking with a senior admiral all tore at Gensoul's professional sense of *honneur*. At 0855hrs, Gensoul signalled his vessels for all crews to take combat stations. As the crews among the Force de Raid scrambled, in a perfect example of understatement, the battleship *Provence* signalled to the destroyer *Volta*, whose crews were scheduled to participate in athletic competitions later that day: 'Impossible to play water polo today.'

At 0905hrs, Holland ordered his boat to make for *Dunkerque* in a bold attempt to try to board the admiral's flagship. He was intercepted in the harbour by Dufay, who again stated that the admiral would not receive the British. Holland then gave Dufay a sealed envelope containing the Admiralty's terms to take to Gensoul. Dufay returned around 1000hrs with a message from Gensoul which reiterated the admiral's previous assurance to Admiral North that his warships would never fall into Axis hands and that, due to the ultimatum he had been presented with, he was prepared to defend his task force if fired upon. Holland then gave Dufay a written personal appeal to Gensoul but, at 1109hrs, Dufay returned, this time with Gensoul's chief of staff, who again stated the admiral's previous message and made clear Gensoul's intention to fight, emphasizing that if the British attacked, the Royal Navy would soon find the entire Marine Nationale arrayed against it. Discouraged, Holland ordered his boat back to *Foxhound*, boarding the destroyer at 1125hrs. The only means by which Holland could report to Somerville was via *Foxhound*'s wireless or signal light, and the limited communication via the coming and going of Holland's and Dufay's boats in the harbour had consumed most of the morning. Thus, by noon, Somerville had only received messages from *Foxhound* that Holland had initiated negotiations and that Gensoul was refusing to meet with him. Somerville had already begun to formulate his own assessment of the situation from reports from *Ark Royal*'s reconnaissance aircraft, however. At 0835hrs, the Swordfish reported that steam was observed coming from the funnels of several vessels, meaning that their boilers had been lit. Subsequent reports stated that the awnings aboard Gensoul's ships were being furled, steam was observed coming from numerous vessels in Oran harbour, and that based upon observation, Gensoul's vessels would be ready for departure at 1230hrs.

With Gensoul's squadron visibly preparing to head to sea, Somerville sent a summary to the Admiralty, which replied at 1045hrs authorizing him to use magnetic mines to block the harbour entrance. As Somerville was weighing his options, based on his very limited information, he

Vice-Amiral Marcel-Bruno Gensoul (right), commander of the Force de Raid at Mers el-Kébir, with his chief-of-staff Capitaine de Vaisseau Jules Julien Lucien Henri Danbé aboard the bridge of Gensoul's flagship *Dunkerque*. (Collection l'Association Amicale des Anciens Marins de Mers-el-Kébir et des Familles des Victimes)

British F-class destroyer HMS *Foxhound*, the vessel which conveyed Captain Cedric Holland to Mers el-Kébir for the negotiations on 3 July 1940. (Author's collection)

finally received a message from Holland at 1227hrs, summarizing his communication exchange and his own observations of the French making preparations for combat and departure. This followed a reconnaissance report that the French battleships were offloading their spotter aircraft, another indication that they were preparing for gunnery combat. With no other recourse immediately available, Somerville ordered *Ark Royal* to fly off five Swordfish bearing magnetic mines and to mine the harbour entrance. He then sent the Admiralty a message of his intention to open fire at 1330hrs. He signalled Holland, asking if there was any alternative to use of force. Holland requested that *Foxhound* make one last communication attempt with Gensoul, asking if he had any message before the British resorted to force. Reluctant to hastily initiate what could be an unnecessary conflict, the admiral readily agreed, deciding to delay a deadline until 1500hrs, and *Foxhound* returned to visual signalling distance with *Dunkerque*. This was a risky move on Somerville's part as this now negated the six hours needed by demolition crews to disable Gensoul's ships before dark, as demanded by the Admiralty's strict timeline. Holland began signalling at 1340hrs and at around 1400hrs signalled a message from Somerville, instructing Gensoul to raise a large square flag at *Dunkerque*'s masthead if he decided to accept any of the British terms, otherwise the British would open fire at 1500hrs. The atmosphere aboard *Foxhound* was tense as the clock ticked and no reply was received from Gensoul's flagship. At 1438hrs, Holland noticed Somerville's warships turned northward, signifying that the battleships were taking up their positions for a long-range bombardment. Finally, at 1440hrs, Holland glanced the blinking of *Dunkerque*'s signal light: Gensoul himself was ready to receive a delegate for 'honourable discussion'. Had the threat of British bombardment convinced the admiral to at last resign himself to bow to *force majeure*?

Fairey Swordfish torpedo bombers taking off from HMS *Ark Royal*. Technically speaking, *Ark Royal* 'fired' the first shots of Operation *Catapult* when five Swordfish dropped magnetic mines across the Mers el-Kébir harbour entrance around 1330hrs on 3 July. (Author's collection)

Quite the opposite; in short, Gensoul needed to buy time. Loyal to Darlan, incensed at what he viewed as the perfidy and insolence of the morning's actions, and unwilling to take any individual initiative other than what his standing orders were, Gensoul had already decided by early morning that he would refuse the British demands. And it increasingly appeared the British were prepared to use force; at 1330hrs, lookouts aboard *Dunkerque* watched as five Swordfish, escorted by six Blackburn Skua fighter-bombers, dropped magnetic mines across the harbour entrance. Nevertheless, he still wanted orders from Darlan regarding the developing situation he found himself in; he did not want to be personally responsible for initiating a shooting conflict with the British. At 0945hrs, after sending alerts to the various naval commands in North Africa, Gensoul sent a message to the Amirauté, now headquartered in Nérac, where it had moved only five days before. Because of the recent move and Axis prohibitions on the use of normal military communications channels, all messages to the Amirauté were routed through the Nérac post office at the time, causing considerable communications delays.

While waiting for instructions from Darlan, Gensoul did prepare his ships for departure, and for combat if he was provoked into action. At 0955hrs, he signalled for all of his vessels to have their boilers lit, although some of his captains had done so already on their own initiative – as observed by *Ark Royal*'s reconnaissance aircraft. Ten minutes later, Gensoul transmitted to his ships, and to Contre-Amiral Marcel Louis Hippolyte Jarry, commander of the other naval forces in Oran: 'English Fleet has come to give us an unacceptable ultimatum, be ready to respond force by force.' Jarry, on his own initiative, ordered his vessels to light their boilers and to prepare for combat. His submarine crews had already begun to disarm their boats' torpedoes, in accordance with the terms of the Armistice of Rethondes, and he ordered them to immediately rearm the weapons, eager to send his submarines to observe the British off the coast. He then contacted the recently demobilized coastal artillery batteries and ordered their crews called up and for the guns to be made operational. Jarry then phoned the commander of the airbase at La Sénia, outside of Oran, and requested that he make any available fighter units operational to provide air cover for Mers el-Kébir and Oran harbour. Gensoul also ordered the four floatplanes, embarked aboard *Dunkerque* and *Strasbourg*, to be lowered into the harbour and to prepare to fly spotting missions for his battleships if the need arose. By noon, Gensoul had put into motion all of the defensive preparations he felt he could; any further actions, other than defending himself if fired upon, needed to come from Darlan.

At 1156hrs, Gensoul's message to the Amirauté was finally received; it read: 'English force including three battleships, an aircraft carrier, cruisers and torpedo boats in front of Oran. Ultimatum sent: sink your boats, delay six hours, or we will compel you to do so by force. Stop. Response: French vessels will respond by force.' The message was given to Vice-Amiral Maurice-Athanase Le Luc, Darlan's chief of staff; Darlan was away from headquarters overseeing yet another Amirauté move, this time to Vichy. Le Luc, on his own authority, immediately phoned the 3ème Escadre at Toulon – composed of the heavy cruisers *Algérie*, *Foch*, and *Colbert* of the 1ère Division de croiseurs, and the 12 destroyers of the 1ère, 3ème, 5ème, and 7ème Division de contre-torpilleurs, commanded by Contre-Amiral Edmond Louis Hyacinthe Derrien – ordering its vessels to immediately light their

French destroyers, from left to right, *Tramontane*, *Tornade*, and *Typhon* of the 7ème Division de torpilleurs moored at Oran in mid-June 1940. Seven destroyers, a torpedo boat, and four submarines based in Oran made preparations to support Amiral Gensoul's squadron during the day on 3 July. (Collection Aubry Palouzier)

French light cruisers *Gloire* and *Montcalm* photographed in Algiers in 1939. They belonged to the 3ème and 4ème Division de croiseurs, based at Algiers under the command of Contre-Amiral Célestin Bourragué, which Darlan ordered to put to sea in order to support Gensoul's Force de Raid. (Author's collection)

boilers. Le Luc then phoned Darlan's present location and ordered Gensoul's message to be delivered at once. At 1255hrs, Le Luc received instructions from Darlan: all Marine Nationale ships in the western Mediterranean were to proceed to Oran and to rally around Gensoul, responding to force with force. Darlan had also sent a message about the situation to the Axis armistice commissions, since Marine Nationale units were required by the terms of the armistice to be demobilized and disarmed. Darlan gambled that an aggressive show of strength against the British would likely be well received by the Germans and Italians.

At 1305hrs, Amiral Le Luc again phoned Toulon, ordering the 3ème Escadre to put to sea when ready and head for Oran. He then sent similar orders to Contre-Amiral Célestin Bourragué, commanding the 3ème and 4ème Division de croiseurs (light cruisers *La Galissonnière*, *Georges Leygues*, *Gloire*, *Jean de Vienne*, *Marseillaise*, and *Montcalm*) at Algiers. At 1405hrs, Le Luc transmitted a message in the clear for Gensoul with orders from Darlan; it would be over two hours before Gensoul received these orders, however. As the uncomfortable silence from the Amirauté continued, Gensoul all the more realized he needed to gain more time to ready his vessels for departure, for submarines – now armed with active torpedoes – to put to sea, for coastal batteries to be mobilized, and for aircraft to be made operational and armed – several hours at minimum. Furthermore, after the aerial mining of the harbour entrance, Gensoul ordered personnel and boats from Marine Oran to make a new opening in the anti-submarine nets that his vessels could escape through – a process of cutting nets and sinking buoys with machine guns, all of which took time. Gensoul also reasoned that if he had to put to sea, it would be best to do so under the cover of darkness. He desperately needed to keep negotiations going with the British until the sun set.

At 1509hrs, *Dunkerque* signalled *Foxhound* that Holland had been granted permission to again enter the harbour and, after a lengthy trip by motorboat, the British captain was finally brought aboard Gensoul's flagship at 1615hrs. As Holland passed by the other battleships along the quay, he could not help but notice the frantic preparations by their crews for getting underway, particularly teams of welders cutting the anchor chains and mooring hawsers as well as tugs waiting at the stern of each vessel to help them turn into the harbour channel. As Gensoul waited to receive Holland, he received one heartening report: several patrols of fighters at La Sénia airfield were either ready to scramble at his request or soon would be; time had allowed for the advantage of fighter cover in the event of combat.

Once aboard, Gensoul quickly made clear to Holland his outrage at the ultimatum and the mining of the harbour, the latter of which he considered an overtly belligerent act. Holland took great lengths to explain the reasoning for the British ultimatum terms but made clear that force would be used if the terms were refused. Gensoul then showed Holland a copy of secret orders, issued by Darlan on 24 June, which stated that if there was any threat of Axis seizure of French warships, commanders were to scuttle their vessels or sail to the West Indies or the United States. As the conversation continued, at 1718hrs Gensoul finally received the 1405hrs message from the Amirauté, with orders from Darlan: 'You will let the British intermediary know that *Admiral de la Flotte* has ordered all French naval forces in the Mediterranean to join you in fighting order. Stop. You have the power to give these forces orders. Stop. You will respond to force with force. Stop. Call in submarines and planes if necessary. Stop. Armistice Commissions otherwise warned.' At last, Gensoul had his orders. Gensoul gave the message to Holland to read and then offered what he considered to be an olive branch, one which might buy a little more time if the British gave it consideration: he would continue to disarm and demobilize his vessels, a solution which in theory would both satisfy the requirements of the armistice and allay British concerns. He then proceeded to write a communication for the captain to send to Somerville:

1. The French fleet cannot do otherwise than apply the clauses of the Armistice, on account of the consequences which would be borne by Metropolitan France.
2. It has received definite orders [*orders formel*], and these orders have been sent on to all commanders, in order that if after the Armistice there is risk of the ships falling into enemy hands, they would be taken to the United States or scuttled.
3. These orders will be carried out.
4. Since yesterday, 2 July, the ships now at Oran and Mers-el-Kébir [*sic*] have begun their demobilization (reduction of crews). Men from North Africa have been disembarked.

With this, there was little more for the officers to discuss and Holland signalled *Foxhound* a summary of Gensoul's note via *Dunkerque*'s signal light. At 1525hrs, however, as Holland prepared to leave *Dunkerque*, Gensoul received a message, transmitted by wireless and signalled directly from Somerville ten minutes before: 'If one of the British proposals is not accepted by 17:30 BST, I must sink your ships.' The time for talk was over.

Unknown to both Gensoul and Holland, at 1614hrs the Admiralty had learned, through Royal Navy monitoring stations, of the 1405hrs Amirauté message regarding naval reinforcements to Gensoul. Aware from a message from Somerville that negotiations between Holland and Gensoul had resumed, First Sea Lord Pound immediately transmitted the French message to Somerville, along with the following instructions: 'Settle the matter quickly or you may have French reinforcements to deal with.' Somerville received this message at 1646hrs and, remembering the Admiralty's strict instructions to conclude the operation before nightfall, immediately began making preparations for an attack. The timing for the attack was hardly ideal; roughly three hours of daylight remained. Furthermore, *Ark Royal* was in no position to launch an immediate air attack. It had been ready to launch bombing strikes for the scheduled attack at 1500hrs, but after a two-and-a-half-hour delay, its 22 aircraft that were currently

Captain Cedric Holland photographed leaving *Dunkerque* at 1725hrs on 3 July at the conclusion of his negotiation attempts. Somerville commenced fire on Gensoul's warships only a half hour later. (© Tous droits réservés Ministère des armées – Mémoire des hommes, Conservé au Musée national de la Marine, Inv. CE 2018.7.1)

Photograph taken from aboard *Dunkerque* around 1800hrs during the Royal Navy bombardment. *Provence* is in the foreground with her turrets trained on the battleships of Force H. *Strasbourg* is behind, just beginning to move away from the quay. In the background is *Bretagne* with smoke coming from around turret no. 4, where two British 381mm shells struck a minute before, causing an internal explosion. (Photo 12/Universal Images Group via Getty Images)

airborne (launched at various times earlier in the afternoon for conducting anti-submarine patrols, reconnaissance, gunnery spotting, and flying fighter cover) were all low on fuel and needed to land. As replacement aircraft would have to also be launched to resume reconnaissance and patrol flights, Somerville was faced with a tough decision: launch a bombing strike against Gensoul's vessels and risk the loss of aircraft low on fuel or delay an attack in order to recover and replace his reconnaissance and patrol aircraft. Somerville therefore decided to initiate the coming fight with a gunnery bombardment alone to recover his aircraft.

Back in Mers el-Kébir harbour, as Holland headed towards the open sea in *Foxhound*'s motorboat, he could hear the battleships calling their crews to action stations and noticed the rear turrets of *Bretagne* and *Provence* turning in the direction of Somerville's battleships. Gensoul was preparing both to fight and to run. At 1730hrs, he ordered the destroyers moored at Saint André to be prepared to immediately cast off and proceed into the channel and out to sea, leading the battleships if the British opened fire. As the clock ticked, many of the French sailors came to believe that the British threat proved to be empty. They had watched as the British vessels turned northward and disappeared into the horizon. Twenty-five minutes since the British deadline had passed and there had been no bombardment; perhaps the Royal Navy had retired. Gensoul and his officers knew better; they reasoned that the British would open fire outside the range of Mers el-Kébir's lighter shore batteries from the north-west, where Fort de Mers el-Kébir would obstruct French return fire. That was exactly what the British would do. After sailing to the north-west, Somerville turned his battleline along a 100° heading at 1753hrs. One minute later, lookouts aboard *Dunkerque* again spotted, although difficult to make out in the late afternoon sun, the silhouettes of the capital ships of Force H. Moments later, the lookouts spotted bright flashes of orange light emerge from the silhouettes. At 1754hrs, at a distance of 16,000m, Somerville ordered his battleships to open fire.

MERS EL-KÉBIR

At 1756hrs, Capitaine de Vaisseau Louis Collinet was standing on the bridge of *Strasbourg* when he heard a distant rumble off to the north-west. Seconds later, his vessel shook from the explosions of 381mm shells, detonating on the nearby breakwater and showering *Strasbourg*'s decks with a lethal rain of concrete shards. After shielding his eyes from the flying debris, he looked to the north-west but could not see the enemy in the distance. Sailing in column at 20 knots 5km away, and firing indirectly over Fort de Mers el-Kébir, *Hood*, *Resolution*, and *Valiant* let loose with full 381mm broadsides, targeting the French capital ships moored along the quay; *Arethusa* and *Enterprise*, ordered to suppress fire from the shore batteries, simultaneously opened fire. After steadying himself from the initial explosions, Collinet was handed a message from Gensoul, which was being relayed across the squadron by flag: 'Cast off without waiting for further signal. Open fire.' Earlier that afternoon, Gensoul had issued instructions that in the event of attack, the destroyers were to sail independently and get out of the harbour as quickly as possible while the battleships were to proceed in the following order: *Strasbourg*, *Dunkerque*, *Provence*, and *Bretagne*. Knowing he was to lead the French charge out of the harbour, at 1758hrs Collinet gave the order to cast off and *Strasbourg* began to turn to port as explosions from the second British 381mm salvo showered further concrete debris upon his ship. Two minutes later, as *Strasbourg* cleared her mooring location, shells from the third British heavy salvo landed directly in the battleship's wake, exactly where she had been a minute before. As water from the explosions sprayed against the bridge windows, Collinet briefly breathed a sigh of relief, not realizing quite how fortunate his vessel had been. Further down the breakwater, the other battleships would not be so lucky.

To *Strasbourg*'s starboard, *Provence* had been the first to respond to the British attack; Contre-Amiral Jacques Félix Emmanuel Bouxin, commander of the 2ème Division de ligne and flying his flag aboard *Provence*, ordered his gunners to open fire just as *Strasbourg* was slipping her remaining mooring lines. *Provence*'s aft no. 4 turret, already tracking *Hood*, fired its first salvo between *Dunkerque*'s masts, startling a number of the flagship's crew on deck. Turrets no. 1, 2, and 3 eventually opened fire as well, and by *Provence*'s tenth salvo, *Hood* had been bracketed by its fire. As *Provence* began its gunnery duel with *Hood*, Bouxin impatiently looked to starboard at *Dunkerque*, still moored to the breakwater. Gensoul's flagship was supposed to be next in line out of the harbour, but it was four minutes into the battle, and it appeared that her crew were making little attempt to get her underway. At 1802hrs, however, four British 381mm shells struck *Dunkerque*, one of which struck the flagship's no. 2 turret and ricocheted off the roof; a fragment from this shell struck the rangefinder for the 340mm guns aboard *Provence*, killing the gunnery officer overseeing its fire against *Hood*. Quickly ascertaining that *Dunkerque* was seriously damaged, Bouxin ordered *Provence* to slip her moorings in order to get underway but then changed his mind on proceeding into the channel in the event *Dunkerque* did get underway. At 1803hrs, just as *Provence* was beginning to pull away from the quay, it was struck aft by a 381mm shell, which exploded in a canvas store near turret no. 5. The explosion started a fire and wrenched loose an armoured plate below the waterline, causing water to rush in. As the temperature in the aft 340mm magazine began to rise due to the fire, the turret crew flooded it as a precautionary measure. With his flagship on fire and beginning to list by the stern, Bouxin ordered *Provence* to be beached to the south between the villages of Roseville and Sainte-Clotilde, where it ran aground at 1836hrs. Shortly after this order, Bouxin's attention turned back to the quay and the fate of the other battleship under his command.

When the British fire began, Capitaine de Vaisseau Louis René Edmond Le Pivain, commander of *Bretagne*, decided that although his vessel was

Photograph taken at 1809hrs, showing the second internal explosion aboard *Bretagne*, which is already listing to starboard. Moments later, the battleship would capsize to starboard. The seaplane carrier *Commandant Teste*, which came through the battle relatively unscathed, is moored to the right of *Bretagne*. (© Tous droits réservés Ministère des armées - Mémoire des hommes, Conservé au Musée national de la Marine, Inv. CE 2018.7.10)

FORCE H BOMBARDMENT OF MERS EL-KÉBIR HARBOUR, 1759HRS, 3 JULY 1940 (PP.48–49)

There are several surviving aerial photographs of Mers el-Kébir harbour during Force H's bombardment, which began at 1756hrs on 3 July, taken by *Dunkerque*'s and *Strasbourg*'s Loire 130 spotter aircraft. They give unique glimpses of events within a naval battle as it was fought. Those photographs inspired this scene, showing the events in Mers el-Kébir harbour at 1759hrs, three minutes after the start of the bombardment. At the left end of the quay, adjacent to Fort de Mers el-Kébir, *Dunkerque* (**1**) is still moored by her stern to the pier and unable to get underway as the deck crew failed to slip the mooring lines prior to taking cover. To the right, *Provence* (**2**) has trained all of her 340mm turrets towards Force H, to the north-west, and has begun to return fire. Next in line, *Strasbourg* (**3**) is just beginning to move forward into the harbour channel. To her right, *Bretagne* (**4**) has just been hit aft by two 381mm shells, one of which causes an internal explosion while the second explodes in her central engine room, causing her to lose power.

to take up position last in the line of battleships exiting the harbour, he had no intention of having his ship remain a sitting target. Immediately, he ordered his crew to cast off and commanded the helmsman to turn hard-a-port; Pivain intended not to immediately proceed into the harbour channel but to turn his vessel directly in front of *Commandant Teste* to port and sail slowly parallel to the channel, allowing all of his batteries to engage the enemy while waiting for the other battleships to pass. As

The wreck of *Bretagne* shortly after capsizing, with her keel still above water. Boats from *Commandant Teste* are patrolling for survivors. *Provence*, in the background and with her turrets pointed towards Force H, is just getting underway across the harbour channel. (© Tous droits réservés Ministère des armées - Mémoire des hommes, Conservé au Musée national de la Marine, Inv. CE 2018.7.15)

with *Strasbourg*, *Bretagne*'s rangefinders found their line of sight towards the British battleships blocked by Fort de Mers el-Kébir, so its turrets did not immediately respond to the incoming fire.

At 1759hrs, just as *Bretagne* was beginning to turn to port, the third British salvo rained down. One 381mm shell penetrated near the base of turret no. 4, causing an internal explosion that shook the entire vessel and emitted a column of smoke, which, according to the British, rose several hundred feet high. Another 381mm shell in the salvo penetrated the hull just aft of the first shell and exploded in the central engine room, knocking out the vessel's power and communications. Water poured into the shell holes and as *Bretagne* began to settle by the rear, Pivain gave orders for his vessel to proceed directly south across the channel and to beach itself along the coast. For several tense minutes, *Bretagne* made no movement forward while developing a list to starboard.

Finally, a message from below was delivered to Pivain; the engines were without power. With the list to starboard increasing and fires spreading from the aft forward, Pivain ordered his crew to abandon ship. Minutes later, two more British shells struck *Bretagne* near turret no. 3, setting off ready-use secondary and anti-aircraft ammunition. At 1809hrs, a second massive internal explosion rocked *Bretagne* and moments later the stricken battleship capsized to starboard. Pivain was thrown into the water as the ship capsized but managed to survive; the majority of his crew, still below decks, were not so fortunate. *Commandant Teste*, to the left of *Bretagne* and which came through the bombardment with only light damage from flying debris, lowered her boats to rescue the battleship's survivors, swimming through clouds of smoke overhead and thick oil in the water. A saving grace of *Bretagne*'s sacrifice was that the explosions that devastated it also blanketed the quay with thick black smoke, partially obscuring the other French vessels from the British fire.

Dunkerque had the most difficulty of all the battleships in getting underway and into action. For the first few minutes of the battle, *Dunkerque* did not open fire as the gunnery officer in charge of her primary turrets

Dunkerque, photographed from *Provence*, beginning to move away from the quay around 1802hrs with her turrets training on Force H. (Collection l'Association Amicale des Anciens Marins de Mers-el-Kébir et des Familles des Victimes)

Photograph showing Gensoul's destroyers getting underway during the bombardment. *Kersaint* (pennant no. X93), which did not depart during the attack due to having only one operable propeller shaft, is to the left. The 381mm shell splashes can be seen around the battleships along the quay in the background. (Collection l'Association Amicale des Anciens Marins de Mers-el-Kébir et des Familles des Victimes)

had not received instructions or a target prior to the British bombardment. Shells from the second British salvo at 1757hrs hit and exploded on the quay directly behind *Dunkerque*, showering the battleship with a rain of rock and concrete debris, and causing its topside crew to take cover. When the order was given to proceed ahead into the channel, those aboard felt a firm lurch; the last remaining mooring cable at the rear of the battleship had not been cut as the deck crew had scattered below, first from the second British salvo and then from *Provence*'s salvos flying directly overhead. Thus, three minutes into the battle, Gensoul's flagship had neither returned fire nor was following *Strasbourg* into the channel, straining helplessly against a mooring line. Finally, at 1759hrs, *Dunkerque*'s primary turrets joined those of *Provence* and began to fire towards the British over Fort de Mers el-Kébir. The atmosphere on *Dunkerque*'s bridge was chaotic, however; the deafening roar of both it and *Provence*'s salvos made the passing of orders almost impossible.

At 1800hrs, the commander of the nearby tug *Estérel* saw *Dunkerque* struggling against the mooring line and moved his boat towards the quay to assist. Two minutes later, *Estérel*'s crew ran down the quay and finally slipped the mooring line, just as a British salvo bracketed *Dunkerque*. As the flagship finally began to gain some forward momentum, it was hit in rapid succession by four 381mm shells. The first shell glanced off the no. 2 turret without exploding while the second passed through the ship's lower hangar and main deck, exiting through the port hull also without exploding. These shells did little damage but the second cut the electrical cables to the rudder, forcing its crew to use an auxiliary motor to manually steer the vessel. The third shell, however, penetrated the armour belt just below the starboard twin 130mm turret, passing through its handling room and exploding in the adjacent medical store room. The shell started a fire in the handling room which caused two 130mm shells to explode, sending smoke into the forward engine room; with the ventilation system disabled, the engine room had to be abandoned. The fourth shell penetrated the starboard armour belt below the waterline, passing through a fuel bunker and into a boiler room, causing fuel to pour into the room. The ensuing explosion ruptured boilers and intakes, sending scalding steam into the adjacent rooms and forcing their evacuation. *Dunkerque*'s turbines and machinery were not seriously damaged but the loss of boiler pressure and power over parts of the vessel meant she could no longer run or fight. The captain decided to limp her towards Saint André, where the village and peninsula would hide it from British sight. Aboard *Dunkerque*'s bridge, surveying the damage to his flagship and looking over to the oily water where *Bretagne*'s survivors were struggling to swim, Gensoul had had enough. At 1810hrs, he ordered his remaining battleships to cease fire and then began signalling Force H the same, requesting that the British likewise cease fire. Three minutes later, *Dunkerque* dropped anchor in the shallow waters just off the piers to the south-west.

French destroyer *Tigre* photographed from shore, making her dash into the Bay of Oran during the British bombardment. The other destroyers that departed before her can be seen in the background, turning to port. (DR, Collection Aubry Palouzier)

The events of the battle were not limited to the battleships along the quay, however. At 1756hrs, mere moments after the British bombardment began, the destroyers moored near Saint André, with their sterns facing the coast and their bows pointed towards the channel, cast off their lines; they were to proceed in single file through the channel and out the harbour entrance, while the battleships were to manoeuvre into the channel. *Mogador* immediately steamed forward, followed by *Volta*, *Le Terrible*, and *Lynx*; *Tigre* was delayed in casting off due to having to raise her starboard anchor while *Kersaint*, with only one working propeller shaft, was ordered to hold back until the battleships passed. As this procession passed down the channel, the destroyer crews saw *Dunkerque*'s and *Strasbourg*'s spotter aircraft, also moored in the harbour, fire up their engines and proceed to take off. At 1758hrs, lookouts aboard *Mogador* spotted the destroyer *Wrestler* at a distance of 15,000m and opened fire with her turrets. A minute later, as she approached the gate through the anti-submarine nets where a path through the British minefield had recently been cleared by tugs and dredgers from Marine Oran, she ceased fire and slowed in order to allow careful manoeuvring through the clearing. As she approached the nets, she was bracketed by a 381mm salvo, with one of the shells slicing through the rear hull and the depth charges stored on her stern. The shell did not explode, but 16 depth charges did, blowing apart the stern. Fortunately, the rear-most magazine did not explode, and the engine room bulkhead withheld the blast, enabling the ship to remain

Aerial photograph taken around 1800hrs over Mers el-Kébir from a Loire 130 spotter aircraft. In the centre foreground, *Mogador*'s stern has just been blown off, with smoke pouring out from it. In the distance to the right along the quay, a tall cloud of smoke is coming from *Bretagne*. (© Tous droits réservés Ministère des armées - Mémoire des hommes, Conservé au Musée national de la Marine, Inv. CE 2018.6.6)

afloat. Disabled, *Mogador* drifted to starboard, and *Volta* swung around her with *Le Terrible*, *Lynx*, and *Tigre* following; it was clear that the British had observed the destroyers trying to escape. Unable to move or steer his vessel, *Mogador*'s commander allowed her to drift to the south and then dropped anchor well clear of the channel.

Shells continued to land around the destroyers but *Volta* and her companions, having reached 30 knots, entered the path through the harbour entrance at 1803hrs,

FRENCH

1. *Dunkerque* (Dunkerque-class battleship)
2. *Provence* (Bretagne-class battleship)
3. *Strasbourg* (Dunkerque-class battleship)
4. *Bretagne* (Bretagne-class battleship)
5. *Commandant Teste* (unique seaplane carrier)
6. *Mogador* (Mogador-class destroyer)
7. *Volta* (Mogador-class destroyer)
8. *Tigre* (Chacal-class destroyer)
9. *Lynx* (Chacal-class destroyer)
10. *Kersaint* (Vauquelin-class destroyer)
11. *Le Terrible* (Le Fantasque-class destroyer)

FORT DE MERS EL-KÉBIR

SAINT ANDRÉ

INCOMPLETE SECTION OF JETTY

10M LINE

ROSEVILLE

▼ EVENTS

1. Force H

1754hrs. Cruising eastward at a heading of 100°, north-north-west of Mers el-Kébir at a distance of 17,500 yards, Force H opens fire.

1804hrs. After firing 36 381mm salvoes, Admiral Somerville orders a ceasefire as return fire from Amiral Gensoul's battleships has ceased.

1806hrs. Due to coastal battery fire and smoke shrouding the harbour, Force H turns westward to a heading of 280° and makes smoke to cover its withdrawal.

2. Dunkerque

1754–1801hrs. *Dunkerque* is unable to get underway due to an aft mooring line which is not slipped.

1759hrs. *Dunkerque* opens fire with 330mm turrets, firing over adjacent Fort de Mers el-Kébir.

1802hrs. With assistance from tug *Estérel*, *Dunkerque* finally slips her mooring line. As she begins to move forward, *Dunkerque* is struck by four 381mm shells, cutting electrical cables and damaging a boiler room, forcing its evacuation and the adjacent engine room.

1803–1813hrs. *Dunkerque* limps across the harbour channel and drops anchor off Saint André at 1813hrs.

1810hrs. Gensoul, aboard *Dunkerque*, signals Force H, requesting a ceasefire.

3. Provence

1758hrs. Waiting to follow *Dunkerque* into the harbour channel, *Provence*'s no. 4 turret, tracking *Hood*, opens fire.

1759–1804hrs. Four of *Provence*'s 340mm turrets engage *Hood*, firing a total of 23 shells at the British battleship. *Hood* is bracketed on *Provence*'s tenth salvo.

1803hrs. Getting underway just after *Dunkerque* is crippled, *Provence* is hit aft by a 381mm shell, causing a fire and flooding.

1804–1836hrs. *Provence* manoeuvres into the harbour channel but listing to the stern, beaches herself off Roseville at 1836hrs.

4. Strasbourg

1758hrs. With orders to lead the breakout of Gensoul's battleships from Mers el-Kébir, *Strasbourg* casts off.

1758–1804hrs. *Strasbourg* manoeuvres into the harbour channel and at 1804hrs begins to pick up speed and heads for the harbour gate.

1809hrs. *Strasbourg* passes through the harbour gate and, increasing to 28 knots, makes for the Cap Canastel channel and then the open sea.

5. Bretagne

1759hrs. *Bretagne* casts off and begins a turn to port to allow all of her turrets to engage the British battleships. At that same moment two 381mm shells hit, causing an internal explosion and knocking out power to the vessel.

1800–1803hrs. With water coming in from the shell holes, *Bretagne* takes on a list to starboard and to the rear.

1803hrs. Two more 381mm shells strike *Bretagne*, setting off ready-use secondary and anti-aircraft ammunition.

1809hrs. *Bretagne* is rocked by a massive internal explosion and capsizes to starboard.

6. French Destroyers

1756–1759hrs. Destroyers *Mogador*, *Volta*, *Le Terrible*, and *Lynx*, moored with their sterns facing Saint André, cast off and begin heading for the harbour gate in that order. *Tigre*, delayed several minutes by having to raise an anchor, eventually follows. With only one functioning propellor shaft, *Kersaint* stays put during the bombardment.

1759hrs. *Mogador* is penetrated by a 381mm shell aft, causing 16 depth charges to explode, blowing off the destroyer's stern. Unable to move or manoeuvre, *Mogador* drifts south of the channel and eventually drops anchor.

1803hrs. After passing the disabled *Mogador*, *Volta*, *Le Terrible*, *Lynx*, and *Tigre* begin sailing through the harbour gate and proceed across the Bay of Oran.

FORCE H BOMBARDMENT OF MERS EL-KÉBIR HARBOUR, 1754–1810HRS, 3 JULY 1940

Having earlier signalled the vessels of Force H the command 'ANVIL' – the code word signifying that hostilities against the French would commence – Admiral Somerville ordered his battleships to open fire on Gensoul's battleships on the late afternoon of 3 July 1940. *Hood*, *Valiant*, and *Resolution* fired in GIC concentration – firing in a fixed time sequence so that each battleship could spot its salvoes while disregarding other ships' salvoes through careful time-keeping – with *Valiant*'s and *Resolution*'s spotter aircraft directing their fire.

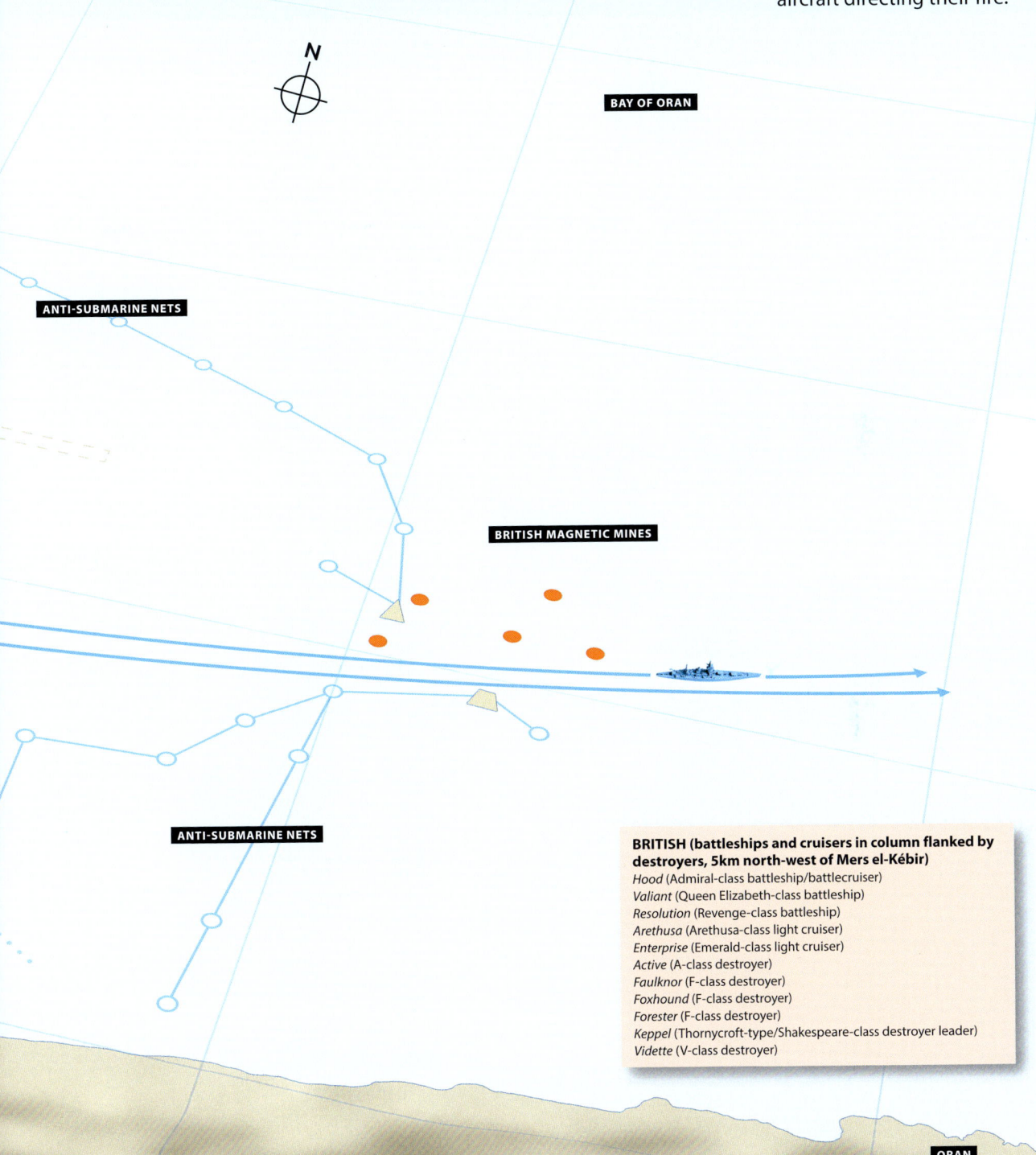

N

BAY OF ORAN

ANTI-SUBMARINE NETS

BRITISH MAGNETIC MINES

ANTI-SUBMARINE NETS

BRITISH (battleships and cruisers in column flanked by destroyers, 5km north-west of Mers el-Kébir)
Hood (Admiral-class battleship/battlecruiser)
Valiant (Queen Elizabeth-class battleship)
Resolution (Revenge-class battleship)
Arethusa (Arethusa-class light cruiser)
Enterprise (Emerald-class light cruiser)
Active (A-class destroyer)
Faulknor (F-class destroyer)
Foxhound (F-class destroyer)
Forester (F-class destroyer)
Keppel (Thornycroft-type/Shakespeare-class destroyer leader)
Vidette (V-class destroyer)

ORAN

dodging the tugs and dredgers still at work. The rain of British shells suddenly stopped a minute later, and the destroyers were able to make their way unmolested through the channel along Cap Canastel, through the defensive minefields, and finally out of the Bay of Oran at 1815hrs. At 1807hrs, the destroyers and torpedo boats in Oran were given orders to cast off and follow the destroyers from Mers el-Kébir through the Cap Canastel channel and out to sea. As the French destroyers emerged from the channel and passed Cap Canastel, they opened fire at long range on the British destroyers *Vortigern* and *Wrestler*, which quickly turned about and disappeared to the north-west into a smokescreen. At 1820hrs, *Volta*'s commander, who was in the lead of the destroyer procession, looked around. There were no British warships visible; only a large smokescreen to the north-west. The route to the north-east into the Mediterranean – and possible escape to Metropolitan France – was wide open.

Out to sea to the north-west of Mers el-Kébir, Somerville had a very limited picture of the events going on within the Bay of Oran. When he ordered the bombardment to commence, his battleline of battleships, cruisers, and six destroyers were sailing in a line eastward. As the wind was blowing from the north-east, *Ark Royal* – with an escort of three destroyers – was sailing in that direction away from Somerville's main force. Lastly, the destroyers *Vortigern* and *Wrestler* had been ordered to take up position further to the east in order to watch the Cap Canastel channel and report on any French vessels attempting to escape. From the outset of the bombardment, Somerville observed that *Hood*'s, *Valiant*'s, and *Resolution*'s fire, guided by spotter aircraft from the battleships and *Ark Royal*, was accurate and causing considerable damage. These aircraft also alerted Somerville to Gensoul's destroyers making their way through the harbour channel and he directed fire accordingly.

This accuracy quickly proved to be a handicap, however. The 381mm hits and the resulting explosions and fires on *Bretagne* and *Mogador* at 1759hrs caused clouds of thick black smoke to envelop the quay and the harbour entrance. As the minutes passed, fire from the larger-calibre coastal batteries started to fall closer to the British battleline. Return fire from the battleships along the quay had noticeably lessened by 1804hrs, however, and Somerville ordered his vessels to cease fire. The increasingly accurate French coastal battery fire and the fact that neither of the battleships' rangefinders nor the spotter aircraft could make accurate observations due to the smoke compelled Somerville to turn the battleline to the west at 1806hrs, and he ordered his vessels to make smoke to mask their withdrawal. The lack of defensive fire coming from the quay caused Somerville to reason that the French battleship crews were in the process of abandoning ship and his temporary ceasefire would allow them to do so without unnecessary loss of life. He then decided that he would proceed westward and manoeuvre into a position where the fire from the coastal batteries would be impeded by the peninsula to the west of the harbour. If by that time Gensoul had

Photograph showing large-calibre shell splashes bracketing *Hood*, either from the 340mm guns of *Provence* or the 240mm guns of Batterie Canastel. Increasingly accurate French defensive fire, and the thick black smoke from *Bretagne* that shrouded the quay, compelled Somerville to cease fire and alter course at 1806hrs. (Author's collection)

not surrendered, fire on the French battleships would be resumed and demolition teams would be disembarked to ensure that they were fully disabled. As his ships sailed away from Mers el-Kébir, Somerville began to receive reports of Gensoul's request for a ceasefire. Somerville ordered the following to be transmitted: 'Unless I see your ships sinking, I shall open fire again.'

At 1820hrs, another report, this time from one of *Ark Royal*'s spotter planes, was handed to the admiral: 'One Dunkerque has left harbour and is going East.' Given Gensoul's repeated requests for a ceasefire and the lack of fire coming from his battleships in the harbour, coupled with several other false reports he had already received during the battle, Somerville believed this report to be false. Furthermore, if French warships were attempting to leave Oran harbour, *Vortigern* and *Wrestler* would have reported the movements. At 1831hrs, however, another report from *Ark Royal*'s aircraft confirmed the previous one: 'Total force at present at sea one Dunkerque and eight destroyers to East of Oran Bay.' A grim realization struck Somerville: a French battleship had broken out of the harbour and was escaping to the east, while the British battleline had been sailing away from them in the opposite direction. Somerville ordered an immediate starboard turn to the east and had *Hood* make full speed. At 1843hrs, he ordered his cruisers and destroyers to the van and eventually *Hood* and its escorts pulled away from the slower *Valiant* and *Resolution*. Leaving his World War I-era dreadnoughts behind, Somerville intended to chase this French battleship down. This was to be a formidable pursuit, however. Unknown to Somerville at the time, his quarry had been sailing to the north-east at 28 knots for 12 minutes while the British battleline had sailed to the west. By the time Somerville's force had completed its eastward turn, the distance between his vessels and the French force was 40km. As he felt the vibrations of *Hood*'s machinery bring the swift battleship up to full speed, Somerville had to wonder: how had one of Gensoul's battleships escaped the bombardment unobserved?

Masked by the clouds of smoke coming from the wrecks of *Bretagne* and *Mogador*, *Strasbourg* miraculously had avoided being hit during the British bombardment and had managed to manoeuvre into the Mers el-Kébir harbour channel at 1804hrs, taking up position behind *Volta*, *Le Terrible*, *Lynx*, and *Tigre*. At 1809hrs, *Strasbourg* reached the harbour gate and slowly manoeuvred through, clearing the nets and mines by a matter of metres. Capitaine Collinet ordered an increase to 28 knots and the battleship raced across the harbour and up the channel along Cap Canastel. Observers spotted the hapless *Wrestler*, making smoke and already under fire from *Volta* and *Le Terrible*, and Collinet ordered his 330mm turrets to engage, firing two salvos. *Wrestler* retreated into the smoke before another salvo could be fired. As *Strasbourg* sailed along Cap Canastel, it was followed northward by the destroyers *Bordelais*, *Trombe*, *Typhon*, *Tornade*, *Tramontane*, *Brestois*, *Boulonnais*, and the torpedo boat *La Poursuivante* from Oran harbour.

By 1825hrs, Collinet had a sizeable escort around *Strasbourg* but noticed to the north-west that the British smokescreen was beginning to dissipate. Expecting the British battleline to emerge from the smoke, Collinet ordered

Photograph taken from the stern of *Volta*, showing *Le Terrible* to the rear, followed by *Lynx* and *Tigre* as the destroyers made their break out of Mers el-Kébir harbour. Note the 381mm shell splash to the starboard of *Le Terrible*. (Jacques Mulard via Wikimedia Commons, CC-BY-SA)

Strasbourg, viewed from Oran, making its dash across the Bay of Oran towards the Cap Canastel channel. The battleship's guns are trained on the British destroyers Vortigern and Wrestler, guarding the exit from the bay. (Collection l'Association Amicale des Anciens Marins de Mers-el-Kébir et des Familles des Victimes)

OPPOSITE

The Curtiss H-75A-1 was the primary Armée de l'Air fighter encountered by Fleet Air Arm aircraft during Operations Catapult and Lever, with Groupes de Chasse I/5 and II/5, based at Saint-Denis-du-Sig airfield, exclusively equipped with the type. American-made, the H-75 was purchased in large numbers by the Armée de l'Air before the war due to delays with domestic French fighter production. This surviving H-75, in the colours of GC II/5 'La Fayette', is preserved in airworthy condition at The Fighter Collection in Duxford, in the United Kingdom. Curtiss H-75A-1 specifications – length: 28ft 6in (8.7m); wingspan: 37ft 4in (11.4m); powerplant: 1,050hp Pratt & Whitney R-1830-SC3-G radial engine; maximum speed: 313mph (504km/h); range: 625mi (1,006km); ceiling: 32,700ft (10,000m); armament: 4x 7.5mm FN-Browning machine guns. (Tony Hisgett via Flickr, CC BY 2.0)

Strasbourg's guns to turn and prepare to engage the enemy. As the smoke continued to clear, however, there were no British ships in visual range; where had the enemy gone? But moments later, Collinet received a signal from Volta, stating a large enemy vessel, likely a battleship or cruiser, was spotted to the north-north-west, just out of range of the destroyer's guns. Gradually, the large vessel came into view at long range in Strasbourg's rangefinder; it appeared to Collinet that he had stumbled upon the British battleline. For several tense moments the French force tracked the large vessel but, at 1840hrs, Strasbourg's lookouts announced that the enemy was turning to the north-west and disappearing into a smokescreen. Collinet was baffled; the British appeared to be in a position to cut him off from escaping into the Mediterranean and had just turned tail and ran. Not willing to question this fortuitous development for long, Collinet kept Strasbourg on its north-eastward course along the Algerian coast and would head east into the Mediterranean once he rounded Cap de l'Aiguille. If his good fortune held up, he hoped to rendezvous with the other Marine Nationale task forces which had been sent to assist Gensoul.

The large British vessel spotted by Volta and Strasbourg happened to be Ark Royal, which was still cruising to the north-east with its destroyer escorts. During the bombardment of Mers el-Kébir, the carrier had been busy recovering aircraft from previous sorties and preparing a strike force which Somerville intended to use as a coup de grâce against Gensoul's damaged battleships. At 1825hrs, when Volta first sighted Ark Royal, the carrier's strike force was finally assembled on deck and cleared for take-off. At 1827hrs, as the strike aircraft were making their way off the flight deck, Vice Admiral Lionel Wells, Vice Admiral, Aircraft Carriers and commanding Ark Royal, received a report from one of his reconnaissance aircraft of a Dunkerque-class battleship and eight destroyers heading east from the Bay of Oran, the message that Somerville received at 1830hrs. Wells quickly consulted a chart and realized that if this report was true, Ark Royal could soon be within gunnery range of a French battleship. Then, at 1835hrs, the lookout aboard Ark Royal's bridge announced a chilling site: stem waves from two fast-moving destroyers spotted to the south-east – Ark Royal was within visual range of the French task force. Wells ordered an immediate turn to the north-west and for Ark Royal to make full speed just as the silhouette of a large enemy vessel came into view, at a distance of 14,000m. As Ark Royal was making its turn, Wells radioed the aerial strike group to abort the attack on the battleships at Mers el-Kébir and to attack the French battleship closing on the carrier. The attack would hopefully force the French into evasive manoeuvres and enable Ark Royal to gain some distance from the French, while at the same time allowing a flight of Swordfish to be armed with torpedoes for a later attack. The battle for Mers el-Kébir was now to take on an aerial dimension.

Around 1830hrs, three Skuas of 803 Squadron's Green Section, led by squadron commander Lieutenant John M. Bruen in Skua L.2927, lifted off Ark Royal. They were tasked with escorting the flight of six Swordfish torpedo bombers from 818 Squadron, each armed with four 250lb SAP bombs and eight 20lb bombs, which Somerville ordered to finish off Gensoul's battleships. Torpedoes would have been much more effective for the job, but the aircraft were unable to make effective torpedo runs due to the ships being moored in close proximity to each other and due to the narrow confines of the harbour. Bruen was fairly new to squadron command, having been promoted when 803 Squadron

Strasbourg firing on *Vortigern* and *Wrestler*, photographed from the armed merchant cruiser *Colombie* in the port of Oran. The British destroyers withdrew behind a smokescreen, allowing *Strasbourg* and its consorts to escape into the Mediterranean. (DR, Collection Aubry Palouzier)

was decimated by Luftwaffe fighter cover in a failed attack on the German battleship *Scharnhorst* off Norway on 13 June 1940. It appeared at first that Bruen's mission would be rather straightforward, as anti-aircraft fire over Mers el-Kébir was reported to be negligible and there had been no French aerial activity so far that day. As Bruen climbed towards the harbour, however, it soon became apparent that the British were no longer alone in the skies. In the distance, Bruen spotted five French Curtiss H-75s diving on one of 820 Squadron's Swordfish, which had been spotting for the battleships. Capitaine Gérard Portalis, leading this patrol from Groupe de Chasse II/5, opened fire on the Swordfish, sending the biplane scurrying back towards *Ark Royal* and its protective anti-aircraft fire. Despite having witnessed first-hand the mauling of his squadron at the hands of Messerschmitt Bf 109 and Bf 110 fighters over Norway only weeks before, Bruen signalled to his flight to engage the attackers and turned to meet the enemy. It was by no means a fair fight; in addition to being outnumbered by the French, the Curtiss H-75 had a maximum speed of 313mph compared to the 225mph of the Skua. Nevertheless, the Skuas swept in on the H-75s. Petty Officer Thomas F. Riddler, piloting Skua L.2915, managed to get onto the tail of the H-75 piloted by Sous-Lieutenant Paul Boudier and opened fire. Boudier went into a tight turn and dived towards the sea, levelling out at 500m. As he spiralled down, Boudier saw to his rear Riddler's Skua go into an uncontrolled spin and crash into the waves; Riddler and his observer, Naval Airman H. T. Chatterley, had the tragic distinction of being the only British casualties in the battle for Mers el-Kébir. Meanwhile, at higher altitude, Bruen and his remaining squadron mate, Sub-Lieutenant Guy W. Brokensha in Skua L.2997, engaged the other H-75s, slightly damaging two of them, but were unable to achieve any kills. Both pilots noted that the French fighters did not aggressively make use of the better performance of their aircraft and after a few minutes turned southward and used their superior speed to disengage. Bruen and Brokensha then

(Left) Sub-Lieutenant Guy W. Brokensha of 803 Squadron. (Author's collection) (Right) The Blackburn Skua, first flying in 1937, was designed to serve as a carrier-borne dive bomber that could also serve in the role of a fighter. While a capable dive bomber and the Fleet Air Arm's first monoplane, the Skua stood little chance against contemporary land-based fighters with its low maximum speed and poor manoeuvrability. Nevertheless, the Skua was the only aircraft embarked upon *Ark Royal* that could perform the duties of a fighter during Operations *Catapult* and *Lever*. Shown here are Skuas of 803 Squadron in their pre-war markings. Blackburn Skua Mk.II specifications – length: 35ft 7in (10.9m); wingspan: 46ft 2in (14m); powerplant: 890hp Bristol Perseus XII radial engine; maximum speed: 225mph (362km/h); range: 760mi (1,220km); ceiling: 20,200ft (6,200m); armament: 5x 0.303in (7.7mm) Browning machine guns (one rear-facing); payload: 1x 500lb (230kg) bomb. (Charles E. Brown/Royal Air Force Museum/Getty Images)

headed off to re-join the Swordfish of 818 Squadron; this was not to be their only encounter with French aircraft, however.

The possibility of significant aerial opposition over Mers el-Kébir had not been seriously considered by the Admiralty when planning Operation *Catapult*, as it was assumed that the units of the Armée de l'Air in North Africa were either largely disorganized or demobilized. Indeed, the French squadrons that had fled from France to North Africa were in the process of rendering their aircraft inoperable – draining fuel tanks, deflating tires, and removing propellers and magnetos – in accordance with Article 5 of the Armistice of Rethondes, and to prevent pilots and aircraft from defecting to the British. Around 1030hrs, Gensoul phoned Colonel Alfred André Rougevin-Baville, the Armée de l'Air commander of the airfield at La Sénia south of Oran, and requested all possible aerial assistance in the event of a British attack. Rougevin-Baville in turn contacted his superior, Général Roger Pennès, commandement des forces aériennes et des forces anti-aériennes de l'Afrique du Nord (AFN) et de la 5ème région aérienne (Commander of the air forces and anti-aircraft forces of North Africa [AFN] and the 5th Air Region), who on his own initiative gave orders to make all of the aircraft in his command combat-ready.

Of Pennès forces based around Oran on 3 June, there were four fighter groups whose aircraft were in various states of readiness and repair: at Saint-Denis-du-Sig airfield, 56km south-east of Mers el-Kébir, was Groupe de Chasse I/5 (Curtiss H-75s) and GC II/5 (Curtiss H-75s); at Relizane airfield, 120km to the east of Mers el-Kébir, was GC II/3 (Dewoitine D.520s and Morane-Saulnier M.S.406s) and GC III/3 (D.520s and M.S.406s). Pennès first contacted Commandants Jacques-Louis Murtin of GC I/5 and Marcel Hughes of GC II/5, ordering them to immediately rearm and ready their fighters. In spite of the shortages of equipment and ground personnel, a three-H-75 patrol was fuelled and armed at 1415hrs; three hours later, 36 of the groups' H-75s were combat-ready. Commandant Jules Morlat and Capitaine Louis Rousseau-Dumarcet of GC II/3 and GC III/3, respectively, received similar orders but these groups had more difficulty in readying their aircraft; nevertheless, several patrols of D.520s and M.S.406s were ready when the British bombardment commenced. The few bombers around the Oran

Force H's pursuit of Strasbourg, 1838–2020hrs, 3 July 1940

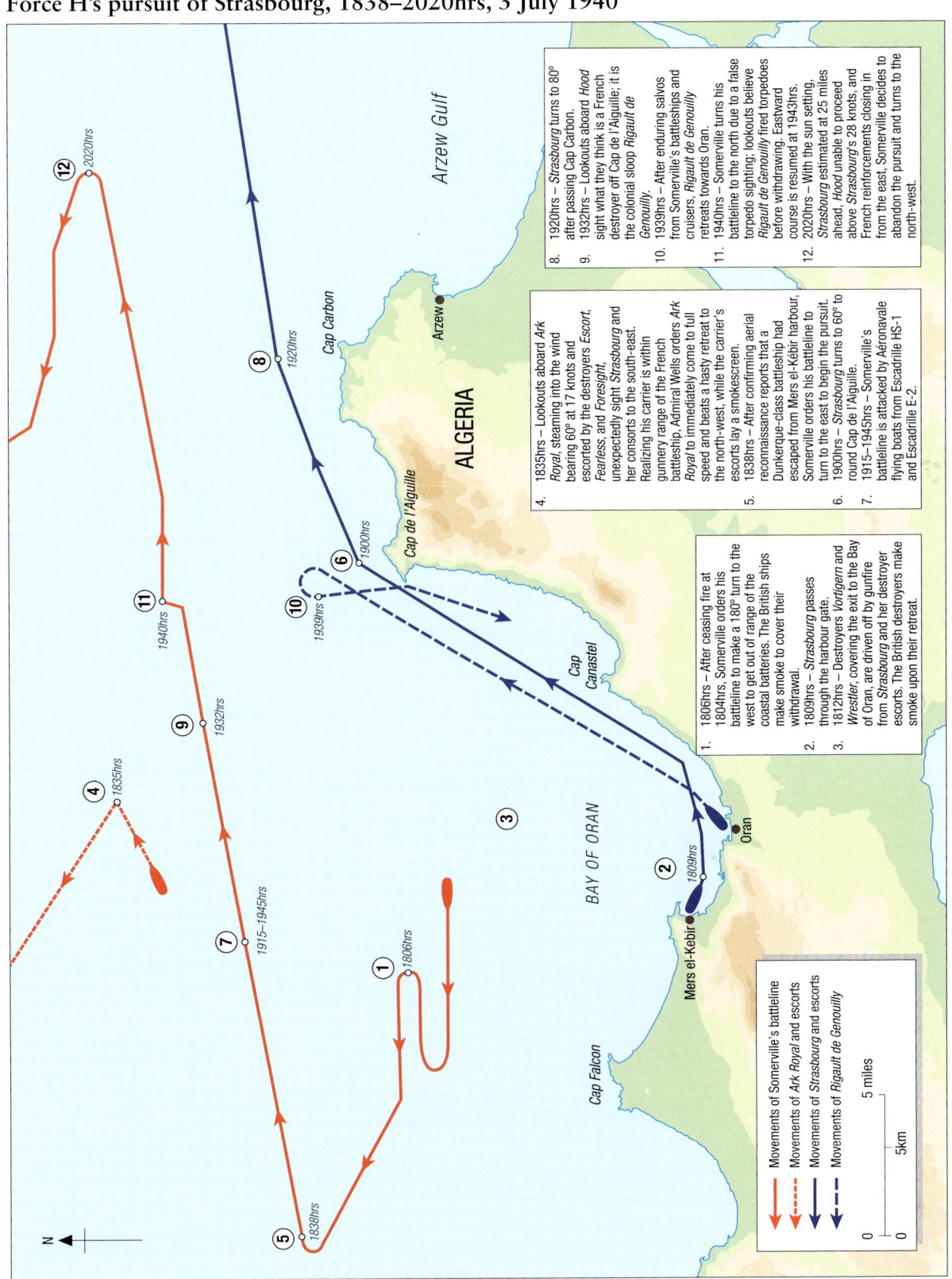

Arzew Gulf

Cap Carbon

Arzew

ALGERIA

Cap de l'Aiguille

Cap Canastel

BAY OF ORAN

Oran

Mers el-Kébir

Cap Falcon

8. 1920hrs – *Strasbourg* turns to 80° after passing Cap Carbon.

9. 1932hrs – Lookouts aboard *Hood* sight what they think is a French destroyer off Cap de l'Aiguille; it is the colonial sloop *Rigault de Genouilly*.

10. 1939hrs – After enduring salvos from Somerville's battleships and cruisers, *Rigault de Genouilly* retreats towards Oran.

11. 1940hrs – Somerville turns his battleline to the north due to a false torpedo sighting; lookouts believe *Rigault de Genouilly* fired torpedoes before withdrawing. Eastward course is resumed at 1943hrs.

12. 2020hrs – With the sun setting, *Strasbourg* estimated at 25 miles ahead. *Hood* unable to proceed above *Strasbourg's* 28 knots, and French reinforcements closing in from the east, Somerville decides to abandon the pursuit and turns to the north-west.

4. 1835hrs – Lookouts aboard *Ark Royal*, steaming into the wind bearing 60° at 17 knots and escorted by the destroyers *Escort*, *Fearless*, and *Foresight*, unexpectedly sight *Strasbourg* and her consorts to the south-east. Realizing his carrier is within gunnery range of the French battleship, Admiral Wells orders *Ark Royal* to immediately come to full speed and beats a hasty retreat to the north-west, while the carrier's escorts lay a smokescreen.

5. 1838hrs – After confirming aerial reconnaissance reports that a Dunkerque-class battleship had escaped from Mers el-Kébir harbour, Somerville orders his battleline to turn to the east to begin the pursuit.

6. 1900hrs – *Strasbourg* turns to 60° to round Cap de l'Aiguille.

7. 1915–1945hrs – Somerville's battleline is attacked by Aéronavale flying boats from Escadrille HS-1 and Escadrille E-2.

1. 1806hrs – After ceasing fire at 1804hrs, Somerville orders his battleline to make a 180° turn to the west to get out of range of the coastal batteries. The British ships make smoke to cover their withdrawal.

2. 1809hrs – *Strasbourg* passes through the harbour gate.

3. 1812hrs – Destroyers *Vortigern* and *Wrestler*, covering the exit to the Bay of Oran, are driven off by gunfire from *Strasbourg* and her destroyer escorts. The British destroyers make smoke upon their retreat.

Movements of Somerville's battleline
Movements of *Ark Royal* and escorts
Movements of *Strasbourg* and escorts
Movements of *Rigault de Genouilly*

5 miles
5km

N

The Fairey Swordfish, first entering Fleet Air Arm service in 1936, was the Royal Navy's primary torpedo bomber in 1940 and remained in service until the end of the war. Lessons learned from the torpedo attacks against *Dunkerque* in Operation *Lever* influenced the highly successful Swordfish attack on the Italian battleships in the Battle of Taranto on 11 November 1940. This Swordfish Mk.II is preserved in airworthy condition by the Navy Wings collection in Ilchester, in the United Kingdom.
Fairey Swordfish Mk.I specifications – length: 35ft 8in (10.9m); wingspan: 45ft 6in (13.9m); powerplant: 690hp Bristol Pegasus IIIM.3 radial engine; maximum speed: 143mph (230km/h); range: 522mi (840km); ceiling: 16,500ft (5,000m); armament: 1x forward-firing .303in (7.7mm) Vickers machine gun, 1x rear-facing .303in (7.7mm) Vickers K machine gun; payload: 1x 1,670lb (760kg) torpedo, 1x 1,500lb (700kg) mine, or 1,500lb of bombs. (Andrew Thomas via Flickr, CC BY-SA 2.0)

area on 3 July were the planes of Escadrilles 2AB and 4AB (Glenn-Martin M.167F) of the Aéronavale at Tafraoui, 24km south of Oran. There were also the reconnaissance aircraft of Groupe de Reconnaissance GR II/52 (Bloch 175) at La Sénia airfield.

The bomber units were not available to Pennès that day, however, as through some mishap in communication, the two Aéronavale squadrons never received an alert on 3 July. For the defensive battle to be fought by Gensoul's warships, however, fighter cover was to be more essential. Early in the afternoon, Pennès received formal authorization from both his superior, inspecteur général de l'Armée de l'air (Inspector General of the Air Force) Joseph Vuillemin, and Pétain's ministre de la Défense nationale (Minister of National Defence) Général Weygand, to make all of the squadrons under his command combat-ready and to accede to any request for air support from Gensoul. When at 1745hrs, Gensoul requested fighter cover, the Armée de l'Air was ready to spring into action.

Back above the Gulf of Oran, the bomb-armed Swordfish from 818 Squadron had been observing the duel between the Skuas and H-75s from a distance when at 1840hrs the flight commander received a wireless message from *Ark Royal*, informing him of *Strasbourg*'s escape. The message further instructed him to scrub the assault on the warships at Mers el-Kébir and to pursue *Strasbourg* and attack it. Bruen and Brokensha also received the message and climbed eastward to re-join the Swordfish. At 1910hrs, as the two Skuas reached 3,600m, they caught sight of the Swordfish flight in the distance. As they approached, Bruen also spotted something ominous to starboard at 4,200m; a group of French fighters appearing to take up position to attack the Swordfish. At 1840hrs, Capitaine Hubert Monraisse had taken off from Saint-Denis-du-Sig with a flight of six H-75s from GC II/5 to relieve Capitaine Portalis' patrol that had encountered the Skuas over the Gulf of Oran. Monraisse was vectored eastward to intercept the British aircraft observed heading towards *Strasbourg*. His flight came up on the Swordfish as the Skuas were approaching, initially unobserved from out of the sun, and he ordered his pilots to take up position behind the bombers but not to open fire until fired upon. A few moments later, Monraisse noted tracers flying past him; although again outnumbered, Bruen and Brokensha swiftly decided to engage the French defenders.

The Skua pilots had the advantage of having the sun to their backs when they made their first pass, firing on the H-75s of Sous-Lieutenant René Trémolet and Sergeants André Legrand and Edouard Sales. Brokensha targeted Trémolet's H-75 and achieved enough hits to force Trémolet to abort combat. Bruen went after Legrand's H-75 but caused no damage. As the Skuas turned to make another attack, Monraisse ordered Legrand, Sales, and Adjutant Paul de Montgolfier to engage the Skuas while he and his wingman, Sous-Lieutenant Paul Marcel Hebrard, intercepted the Swordfish. Legrand then managed to get on Brokensha's tail, firing on the Skua while also dodging the defensive fire from the rear turret. Moments later, Bruen, evading the other fighters, swept in on Legrand and the Frenchman soon found himself being fired on from ahead and astern. Legrand broke off the fight and dived towards the sea. It was discovered after this sortie that three machine guns had jammed on each Skua during this brief but furious engagement.

Further to the east, Monraisse and his wingman intercepted the Swordfish flight but did not engage as they were not fired upon. Around 1940hrs, the Swordfish caught up to *Strasbourg* and the six bombers went into a dive and released their bombs at 1,200m. Unfortunately for their crews, all of the bombs missed, and they promptly found themselves in a sudden storm of anti-aircraft fire. *Strasbourg*'s anti-aircraft crews were also under strict orders not to fire until attacked, and fire was held until the Swordfish released their bombs. The slow-moving biplanes made relatively easy targets for *Strasbourg*'s gunners and two Swordfish were quickly shot down; their crews were later picked by the destroyer *Wrestler*. The four remaining Swordfish managed to escape and the anti-aircraft fire compelled Bruen, Brokensha, and their French opponents to retire.

Back aboard *Hood*, Somerville was becoming increasingly frustrated. In addition to the unlikely eventuality that one of his primary targets, *Strasbourg*, had escaped from the bombardment, his force had also just encountered a bombing attack by a group of antiquated French flying boats (see battlescene on pp.64–65 for details) – hardly a display of the abysmal morale the Admiralty had assured him of within the French naval forces. These were not to be the only instances of unexpected *élan* from his adversaries that evening, however. At 1932hrs, while directly north of Cap Canastel, *Hood*'s lookouts reported an enemy destroyer, just off the coast. It was the colonial sloop *Rigault de Genouilly*, commanded by Capitaine de Frégate Louis Frossard, which was attempting its own breakout to the east from Oran harbour. Frossard's sloop could only make 15.5 knots but, as the British had not fired since 1810hrs and had departed to the west, he assumed the enemy had withdrawn. At 1933hrs, Frossard heard a rumble to the north-west and soon shells were splashing down around his vessel; *Hood*, *Valiant*, *Arethusa*, and *Enterprise* had all opened fire. Frossard began evasive manoeuvres, while turning back towards Oran, and ordered his three

French destroyer *Mogador*, photographed after sustaining critical damage during the 3 July bombardment, moored adjacent to Fort de Mers el-Kébir. (Collection Aubry Palouzier)

AÉRONAVALE ATTACK ON SOMERVILLE'S BATTLELINE, 1940HRS, 3 JULY 1940 (PP.64–65)

As *Ark Royal*'s Skuas duelled with the H-75s from GC II/5, to the west aboard *Hood*, lookouts spotted incoming enemy aircraft. The land-based bombers of the Armée de l'Air may have been unable to attack the British fleet, but the Aéronavale responded to Gensoul's requests for air support. Shortly after the British bombardment began, Marine Oran ordered its reconnaissance squadrons based at Arzew, 32km north-east of Oran, to arm their aircraft and to engage the enemy. Beginning at 1805hrs, the six Loire 130 flying boats of Escadrille HS-1 took off, each carrying two 75kg bombs. They were followed ten minutes later by the two large Bréguet 521 Bizerte three-engine flying boats of Escadrille E-2, each carrying six 75kg bombs. Slow and unwieldy, the flying boats were ordered to bomb Somerville's battleline from a high altitude. It was a desperate effort, made by aircraft unsuited for the mission, but it was hoped the attack would force the British into evasive manoeuvres and perhaps put a little more distance between the British and the French vessels escaping to the east. Beginning at 1915hrs, the Loire 130s released their bombs over *Hood* and her consorts. As the flying boats lacked bombsights, it was merely a dramatic show of resistance. Despite the heavy anti-aircraft fire, none of the Loire 130s were seriously damaged and all returned to Arzew.

At 1940hrs, Bréguet 521 E2-3 dropped its six bombs over the destroyer *Wrestler* (**1**) and managed an uneventful return to base. Then, Bréguet 521 E2-1, commanded by Lieutenant de Vaisseau Remi Duval, released its bombs over the destroyer, some actually landing within 50 metres of the vessel, and escaped the bursting clouds of flak. As Duval flew towards Arzew, he happened upon Bruen and Brokensha, both heading back to *Ark Royal*. Duval began evasive manoeuvres and the flying boat's crew took to the five 7.5mm machine guns as the Skuas circled around their intended prey. Despite being low on fuel, low on ammunition, and with several of their aircrafts' machine guns out of action, Bruen and Brokensha could not resist such an easy target. They made two passes on the flying boat, and on the second, one of the engines was knocked out. Content with this result, the Skua pilots turned towards *Ark Royal*, ending a rather frantic sortie. With an engine out and gasoline trailing from leaking tanks, Duval nevertheless managed to coax his aircraft down onto the waters off Oran and then, with its hull leaking like a sieve, drove it up onto the beach. Upon examination, Duval counted 44 bullet holes in the flying boat; a fortuitous escape. Seen here, Bréguet 521 E2-1 (**2**), piloted by Lieutenant de Vaisseau Duval, takes evasive action as Sub-Lieutenant Brokensha (**3**) in Blackburn Skua L.2997 flies past after attacking the flying boat.

138mm guns to open fire. This unbalanced engagement lasted six minutes, towards the end of which *Rigault de Genouilly* was bracketed and then hit in its forward funnel and boat deck.

At 1939hrs, just as it appeared the little gunboat was to be blown out of the water, *Hood*'s lookouts reported torpedo wakes off the starboard bow. The British ships made a hard turn to port and ceased firing on the sloop. Somerville was astonished; had this little David attempted a torpedo attack against his Goliath? Amazingly, it turned out that the torpedo alarm had been a false sighting; *Rigault de Genouilly* was not armed with any torpedoes. Yet, as he saw the British force suddenly cease fire and swing to the north at 1940hrs, Frossard ordered a hasty retreat; he had taken on the British fleet and had miraculously survived. When Somerville's warships turned back on an eastward heading at 1943hrs, fire was not resumed on *Rigault de Genouilly*. Somerville was focused on a harsh realization: the sun was setting, *Strasbourg* was kilometres outside of gunnery range and getting away, and he had just lost precious minutes dodging what proved to be phantom torpedoes. His only option to stop *Strasbourg* in the fading light was by aerial assault. He ordered *Ark Royal* to launch a torpedo strike against his elusive quarry.

Admiral Wells already had a flight of six Swordfish from 820 Squadron armed with torpedoes when Somerville gave the order for the sunset strike. At 1950hrs, Lieutenant Commander Guy B. Hodgkinson, commander of 820 Squadron, led his flight off *Ark Royal* and headed eastward. The Swordfish flew 24km off the coast until they spotted *Strasbourg* and its consorts steaming to the north-east. The battleship was easy to find; a piece of debris had damaged an air intake on its funnel during the bombardment, resulting in a column of black smoke that could be seen for kilometres. Hodgkinson then led his flight past the French force, having decided to attack from the east when the sun had set, helping to mask his approach and showing *Strasbourg*'s silhouette still just visible against the sun's afterglow. At 2030hrs, just as the sun dropped below the horizon, *Le Terrible* signalled *Strasbourg*, reporting enemy aircraft to the north, flying low and parallel to the French force, heading east. The anti-aircraft batteries on the ships opened fire but the aircraft were soon out of range and disappeared into the darkness.

Ten minutes later, the Swordfish proceeded in a semicircle to starboard and then began to approach the battleship off its starboard bow. Flying in a line and spaced 300 yards apart, the Swordfish then dropped to 20ft to begin

Colonial sloop *Rigault de Genouilly*, photographed in Shanghai before the war. This small warship survived a chance encounter with Force H's battleships and cruisers on the evening of 3 July, only to be sunk by the British submarine *Pandora* the following day off Algiers. (Author's collection)

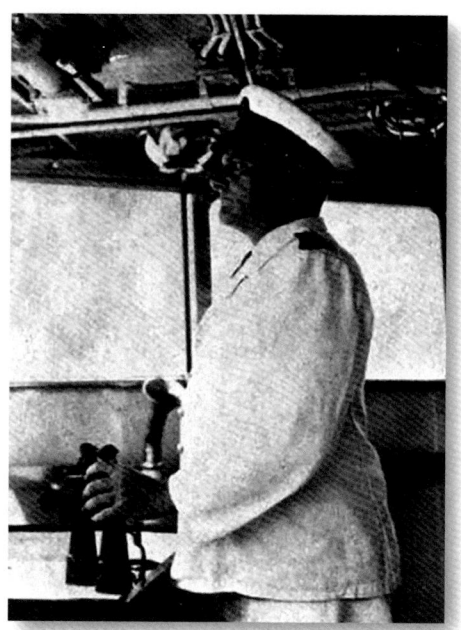

Capitaine de Vaisseau Louis Collinet, *Strasbourg*'s commander, standing on her bridge. Collinet's daring escape to Toulon became a proud achievement for the Marine Nationale in the midst of the Mers el-Kébir disaster. (Collection l'Association Amicale des Anciens Marins de Mers-el-Kébir et des Familles des Victimes)

their torpedo run at 2050hrs. Their approach was not seen by the French until after the torpedoes had been dropped and the aircraft banked away. A lookout aboard the torpedo boat *La Poursuivante* spotted torpedo wakes headed for *Strasbourg* and the battleship was warned. Collinet ordered a hard turn to port as a torpedo bore down upon his vessel. The torpedo passed just aft of the ship and then exploded 25m off the port quarter; Collinet had just escaped a second British trap. As the Swordfish disappeared to the west, Collinet signalled *Volta*, *Le Terrible*, *Tigre*, and *Lynx*, ordering them to sail to the north-east until midnight and then turn to the north with Toulon being their ultimate destination, per instructions received from Darlan at 2010hrs; by maintaining radio silence, Collinet hoped to disappear from the British during the night and arrive in the safety of the Marine Nationale's largest Mediterranean base later on 4 July. Now that Collinet could catch a breath, he reflected on a message he had received at 2025hrs from his spotter plane, which had been sending *Strasbourg* reconnaissance reports since just after the Swordfish bombing strike: pursuing British forces had reversed course and were headed to the west. With a sigh of relief, and with darkness closing in around his ship, Collinet ordered his crew to stand down from their action stations and instructed for supper to be served; they had gotten away.

Indeed, as the sun was setting, at 2020hrs Somerville ordered *Hood* and its consorts to give up the chase and to turn towards the west; he had run out of time. *Hood*, the only ship in his pursuing force capable of taking on *Strasbourg* in a gunnery duel, was only making 28 knots, the same speed as *Strasbourg*; as the French force was maintaining that speed and still 40km ahead, there was no chance of catching up to it, especially once darkness set in. Somerville had also just received intelligence reports from the Admiralty that, based on *Strasbourg*'s last reported course, Amiral Bourragué's six light cruisers from Algiers would rendezvous with the battleship sometime after 2100hrs, creating a force that could easily overpower Somerville's. In his later report to the Admiralty, Somerville formally gave the following reasons for abandoning the pursuit:

- The prospects of locating and engaging the French battlecruiser at night were small.
- Force 'H' would be at a disadvantage, being silhouetted against the afterglow.
- The speed of advance was too high to allow the destroyers to spread.
- The fuel endurance of the 'V' and 'W' class destroyers would not permit of more than three hours' chase.
- Unless *Hood* was in a position to support the advanced forces, the latter would be numerically much inferior to the French. This support could not be assured under night action conditions.
- I did not consider that the possible loss of British ships was justified as against the possibility of French ships being allowed to fall into German or Italian hands.
- *Valiant* and *Resolution* were unscreened.

Force H aerial attacks on *Strasbourg*, 1825–2055hrs, 3 July 1940

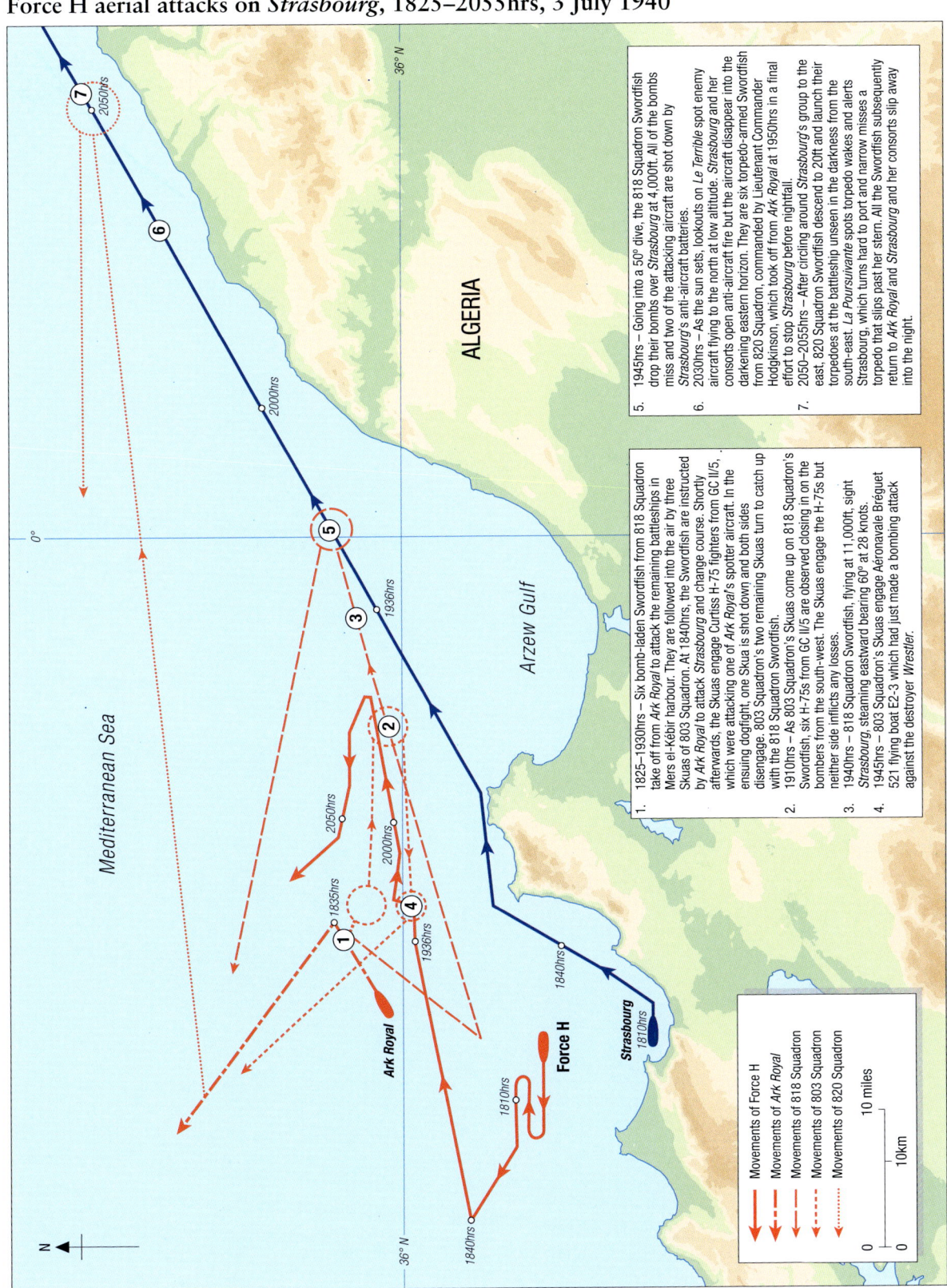

1. 1825–1930hrs – Six bomb-laden Swordfish from 818 Squadron take off from *Ark Royal* to attack the remaining battleships in Mers el-Kébir harbour. They are followed into the air by three Skuas of 803 Squadron. At 1840hrs, the Swordfish are instructed by *Ark Royal* to attack *Strasbourg* and change course. Shortly afterwards, the Skuas engage Curtiss H-75 fighters from GC II/5, which were attacking one of *Ark Royal*'s spotter aircraft. In the ensuing dogfight, one Skua is shot down and both sides disengage. 803 Squadron's two remaining Skuas turn to catch up with the 818 Squadron Swordfish.

2. 1910hrs – As 803 Squadron's Skuas come up on 818 Squadron's Swordfish, six H-75s from GC II/5 are observed closing in on the bombers from the south-west. The Skuas engage the H-75s but neither side inflicts any losses.

3. 1940hrs – 818 Squadron Swordfish, flying at 11,000ft, sight *Strasbourg*, steaming eastward bearing 60° at 28 knots.

4. 1945hrs – 803 Squadron's Skuas engage Aéronavale Bréguet 521 flying boat E2-3 which had just made a bombing attack against the destroyer *Wrestler*.

5. 1945hrs – Going into a 50° dive, the 818 Squadron Swordfish drop their bombs over *Strasbourg* at 4,000ft. All of the bombs miss and two of the attacking aircraft are shot down by *Strasbourg*'s anti-aircraft batteries.

6. 2030hrs – As the sun sets, lookouts on *Le Terrible* spot enemy aircraft flying to the north at low altitude. *Strasbourg* and her consorts open anti-aircraft fire but the aircraft disappear into the darkening eastern horizon. They are six torpedo-armed Swordfish from 820 Squadron, commanded by Lieutenant Commander Hodgkinson, which took off from *Ark Royal* at 1950hrs in a final effort to stop *Strasbourg* before nightfall.

7. 2050–2055hrs – After circling around *Strasbourg*'s group to the east, 820 Squadron Swordfish descend to 20ft and launch their torpedoes at the battleship unseen in the darkness from the south-east. *La Poursuivante* spots torpedo wakes and alerts *Strasbourg*, which turns hard to port and narrow misses a torpedo that slips past her stern. All the Swordfish subsequently return to *Ark Royal* and *Strasbourg* and her consorts slip away into the night.

Later that evening, Somerville received a signal, sent by Gensoul at 2135hrs: 'Warships at Mers el-Kébir out of action due to damage. I am evacuating crews from warships.' This reassured Somerville of his decision to head westward.

Despite Gensoul's message, there was one nagging detail: had Gensoul's remaining battleships in Mers el-Kébir actually been destroyed or disabled? Aerial reconnaissance had confirmed the sinking of *Bretagne* but were *Provence* and *Dunkerque* actually rendered, as quoted by Gensoul, *hors de combat*? As his primary instructions had been to ensure the disabling and destruction of *Dunkerque* and *Strasbourg*, and as the latter had gotten clean away, Somerville was intent on ensuring that *Dunkerque* was definitively neutralized. He signalled the vessels of Force H to rendezvous at a position roughly 97km to the west-north-west of Oran, where they would take up station for the night. He then intended to launch a final airstrike from *Ark Royal*, made up of 12 Swordfish and nine Skuas, at dawn to ensure that Gensoul's battleships were indeed finished off. During the night, however, thick fog set in and at 0400hrs on 4 July, a half hour before the scheduled airstrike, Admiral Wells advised Somerville to call off the operation as his aircrews would not be able to navigate or attack with such low visibility. With his destroyers beginning to run low on fuel due to the attempted high-speed pursuit of *Strasbourg*, Somerville ordered Force H to return to Gibraltar, which was reached at 1900hrs that day. For the moment, Gensoul's word regarding the fate of his battleships in Mers el-Kébir would have to suffice.

GREAT BRITAIN AND ALEXANDRIA

Dreadnought battleship *Paris* photographed in Plymouth, flying the Union Jack, following her seizure by the Royal Navy. Due to her advanced age and heavy crew requirements, she was not put into active service by either the Royal Navy or Free French movement, and spent the remainder of the war as a depot and barracks vessel. (Naval Heritage and History Command NH 889850)

As mentioned previously, Gensoul's battleships at Mers el-Kébir were not the only objectives of Operation *Catapult* on 3 July. The first targets of the day were the Marine Nationale vessels moored in ports in Great Britain. In the preceding days, the Admiralty used various pretences to vector most of the French warships into Plymouth and Portsmouth harbours. On 2 July, the Royal Navy admirals in those ports were given orders to assemble boarding parties during the night and, through an overwhelming show of force at dawn, rapidly seize the warships peaceably or by force if necessary. Boarding parties were formed from sailor complements from Royal Navy warships in the harbours or detachments of Royal Marines. At 0430hrs on 3 July, Admiral Martin Dunbar-Nasmith, Commander-in-Chief, Plymouth and Western Approaches, began the operation in Plymouth harbour, personally leading a boarding detail aboard the battleship *Paris*. Vice-Amiral Lucien Cayol, commander of the French vessels in Plymouth, was roused from his bunk to find British sailors and marines swarming throughout the battleship. Dunbar-Nasmith diplomatically explained the action to Cayol, who bowed to *force majeure* and instructed his men not to resist. Simultaneously with the seizure of *Paris*, across Plymouth and Portsmouth harbours, boarding parties quickly swept aboard the

French vessels and in almost every instance met no resistance from the French crews, other than harsh rebukes.

The notable exception was the boarding of the large submarine cruiser *Surcouf*. When Commander Denis Sprague, skipper of the submarine *Thames*, and his party of 60 sailors and marines came aboard *Surcouf*, one of the sentries, while sounding the alarm, fled into the fore hatch and closed it behind him. Finding all of the hatches closed and locked, Sprague ordered his crew to force open the hatch on the conning tower, which could be opened from the outside by divers in the event of a rescue operation. As Sprague and his men spread throughout the submarine, they initially met no resistance but found the crew in a hostile mood. *Surcouf*'s captain asked to consult with Amiral Cayol before handing over his boat and was escorted away.

The unique cruiser submarine *Surcouf*, armed with two 203mm/50 Modèle 1924 guns in a turret mounted in front of the conning tower, photographed arriving in Plymouth on 20 June 1940. A brief firefight between the submarine's officers and a Royal Navy boarding party resulted in the only casualties during the seizure of French warships in British ports on 3 July. (DR, Collection Aubry Palouzier)

During the tense moments of his absence, one of *Surcouf*'s electricians tripped the boat's breakers and in the darkness the engineering officer ran to his cabin and began destroying the submarine's technical manuals. Once power was restored, Sprague ordered *Surcouf*'s officers off the boat, but they refused and several quietly armed themselves. When Sprague threatened to shoot a truculent French officer, another drew a pistol and a brief firefight broke out in the close confines of the officers' wardroom and cabins. When the smoke had cleared, Sprague, another British officer, a British sailor, and *Surcouf*'s engineering officer were dead or dying. *Surcouf*'s officers then surrendered and were escorted off the submarine with the remainder of the crew. They, along with the crews of the other French warships seized, were sent to internment camps where conditions were poor, and they were denied correspondence with relations in France. Eventually, towards the end of 1940, these crews were offered repatriation to the unoccupied zone of France and the majority returned. Not surprisingly, especially after learning of the events at Mers el-Kébir, few officers and sailors chose to join Général de Gaulle's Free French movement.

The neutralization of the warships of French Force X in Alexandria harbour proved to be the most successful episode in Operation *Catapult* for the British. On the evening of 24 June, Amiral Godfroy had received coded instructions from Darlan to immediately sail Force X to a French port due to the armistice about to begin. On instructions from the Admiralty, Admiral Cunningham denied Godfroy's request to depart the following day. As the two admirals had maintained a cordial relationship, a détente was worked out in which Cunningham promised not to seize Godfroy's vessels provided the French stayed put; Godfroy even offered to remove the fuel from his vessels as a cooperative gesture and repeatedly mentioned his desire to continue fighting alongside the Royal Navy. Churchill, however, was irritated with the initiative shown by Cunningham in this matter. The Prime Minister had decided that he wanted to gain control of Force X's vessels, particularly the battleship *Lorraine* and heavy cruisers *Duquesne*, *Suffren*, and *Tourville*, for British use; they were the most powerful and modern French vessels in a British port and the possibility of easily adding them to

Gunnery practice aboard a Royal Navy Mediterranean Fleet vessel in Alexandria harbour in May 1940. The French dreadnought battleship *Lorraine* is in the background to the right. Admiral Cunningham successfully negotiated the demilitarization of *Lorraine* and the other warships of the Marine Nationale's Force X on 4 July. (Roger Viollet via Getty Images)

the Royal Navy's roster proved very tempting to Churchill. He insisted that the Admiralty add Force X to the list of targets for Operation *Catapult* and Cunningham was ordered to issue Godfroy an ultimatum at 0700hrs on 3 July. The terms of this ultimatum were different than that issued to Gensoul at Mers el-Kébir: Godfroy could either 1. Willingly hand his warships over to the Royal Navy for wartime use; 2. Demobilize and disarm his warships in Alexandria, to be maintained by skeleton crews for the duration of the conflict; or 3. Scuttle his vessels at sea. If Godfroy refused these options, Cunningham was instructed to put to sea with the Mediterranean Fleet and sink Force X in Alexandria harbour. Cunningham thought this action to be absurd as a bombardment from the sea would undoubtedly damage harbour facilities and sunken French vessels would hamper the use of the harbour. Wondering personally to himself if the Admiralty had gone mad, Cunningham nevertheless invited Godfroy aboard his flagship at 0700hrs on 3 July.

Under the awkward circumstances, Godfroy initially took the demands in stride, intimating that he understood the difficult position that the Royal Navy now found itself in. He hinted that he might be willing to accept the terms regarding demobilization and returned to consult with his commanders. In the early afternoon, Godfroy told Cunningham that he would have to scuttle his vessels, unless he could receive instructions from the Amirauté. He further explained that he would recommend to his superiors that his vessels be demobilized and requested 48 hours to make arrangements for the bulk of his crews to go ashore; in return, Godfroy offered to begin defueling his ships and to offload ammunition. Cunningham reported this development to the Admiralty, but that evening received a reply instructing him to begin removing the French crews before dark. The message ended, 'Do not, repeat NOT, fail'; this was Churchill, making it clear that he wanted the situation in Alexandria resolved to his liking before Godfroy learned of the fiasco at Mers el-Kébir. This was not to be the case; Cunningham, who received what he viewed as a petulant message already after dark, deferred any further action until the following day.

On the next morning, Godfroy had finally received orders from the Amirauté, instructing him to immediately put to sea and to fight his way out of Alexandria if need be. Initially, Godfroy was baffled by such a suicidal order, but in a subsequent message he learned of the events of Mers el-Kébir and understood its desperate rationale. Godfroy immediately halted the defueling efforts, informed Cunningham that he was no longer bound by any previous agreements, and signalled his ships to raise steam. When apprised of this development, the Admiralty ordered Cunningham to put to sea and to threaten Force X with destruction if it did not surrender. Cunningham did no such thing; instead, he had his vessels signal the French warships, explaining the current situation and emphasizing his desire to avoid bloodshed. Furthermore, he sent his captains to visit each of the French ships to reason individually with their commanders. His diplomatic approach worked; later that afternoon, Godfroy met with Cunningham and said he would bow to *force majeure*. In private, both admirals agreed that the frenzied courses of action recommended by their respective superiors would only lead to pointless butchery. Cunningham promised to make no attempt to seize the French ships and Godfroy ordered the defueling to be completed, and for the breech blocks of his ships' guns and firing pins of their torpedoes to be sent ashore and stored at the French consulate. This arrangement was formalized on 7 July, where it was agreed the warships would be maintained in Alexandria by reduced crews. Ironically, Churchill offered Cunningham praise for his handling of the ordeal after the fact.

THE IMMEDIATE FRENCH RESPONSE

Meanwhile in Vichy, there was no satisfaction with the course of events in Alexandria as far as Darlan was concerned. In the admiral's mind, the demobilization of Force X was yet another setback in settling scores with *La perfide Albion*. Throughout the afternoon and evening of 3 July, bits and pieces of reports trickled in to Darlan of British seizures of French warships, British ultimatums, and British attacks. Due to the still chaotic state of the Marine Nationale's communications network and that the Amirauté was in the process of transferring from Nérac to Vichy, there were significant time lapses between reports coming in and orders being sent out. This greatly hampered Darlan's strategic understanding and control over the events unfolding in Mers el-Kébir, Alexandria, and Great Britain – and greatly added to his frustration. To say that Darlan was upset with the course of events would be a gross understatement. His reaction is best summed up by a general order he sent to all Marine Nationale commands at 2030hrs on 3 July: 'In view of the hostile attitude taken by the British Royal Navy at Mers el-Kébir, consider it hostile and attack any British warship encountered – The order applies to all surface vessels, submarines, and aircraft – Seize any British merchant vessel encountered and take it to a French port.' On his own initiative, an enraged Darlan had personally declared war on the Royal Navy. When he learned of Gensoul's ongoing communications with Force H during the evening of 3 July, he fired off a sharp rebuke to Gensoul at 2153hrs: 'Stop parleying with the enemy – stop – reference your 2030/3/7 (message) if it is authentic 2153/./7.' The '2030/3/7' message Darlan referred to was his 2030hrs general order. He did not want Gensoul to negotiate; he wanted the admiral to fight – the message was clearly an outburst of frustrated rage. This was Darlan's state of mind when he then sent the message to Godfroy, instructing him to fight his way out of Alexandria.

As more detailed information came in throughout the evening of 3 July regarding the status of Gensoul's battleships still in Mers el-Kébir and the escape of *Strasbourg*, he was able to formulate more organized plans for retaliation, other than simply demanding his subordinates to attack. After learning that

Heavy cruiser *Foch* in the centre, at sea with her sisters. *Foch* was one of the vessels of the 3ème Escadre at Toulon, commanded by Contre-Amiral Edmond Derrien, which Darlan ordered to sea on the evening of 3 July to reinforce Collinet's *Strasbourg* group and Amiral Bourragué's cruisers from Algiers. (Author's collection)

Marine Nationale deployments against Force H, 3–4 July 1940

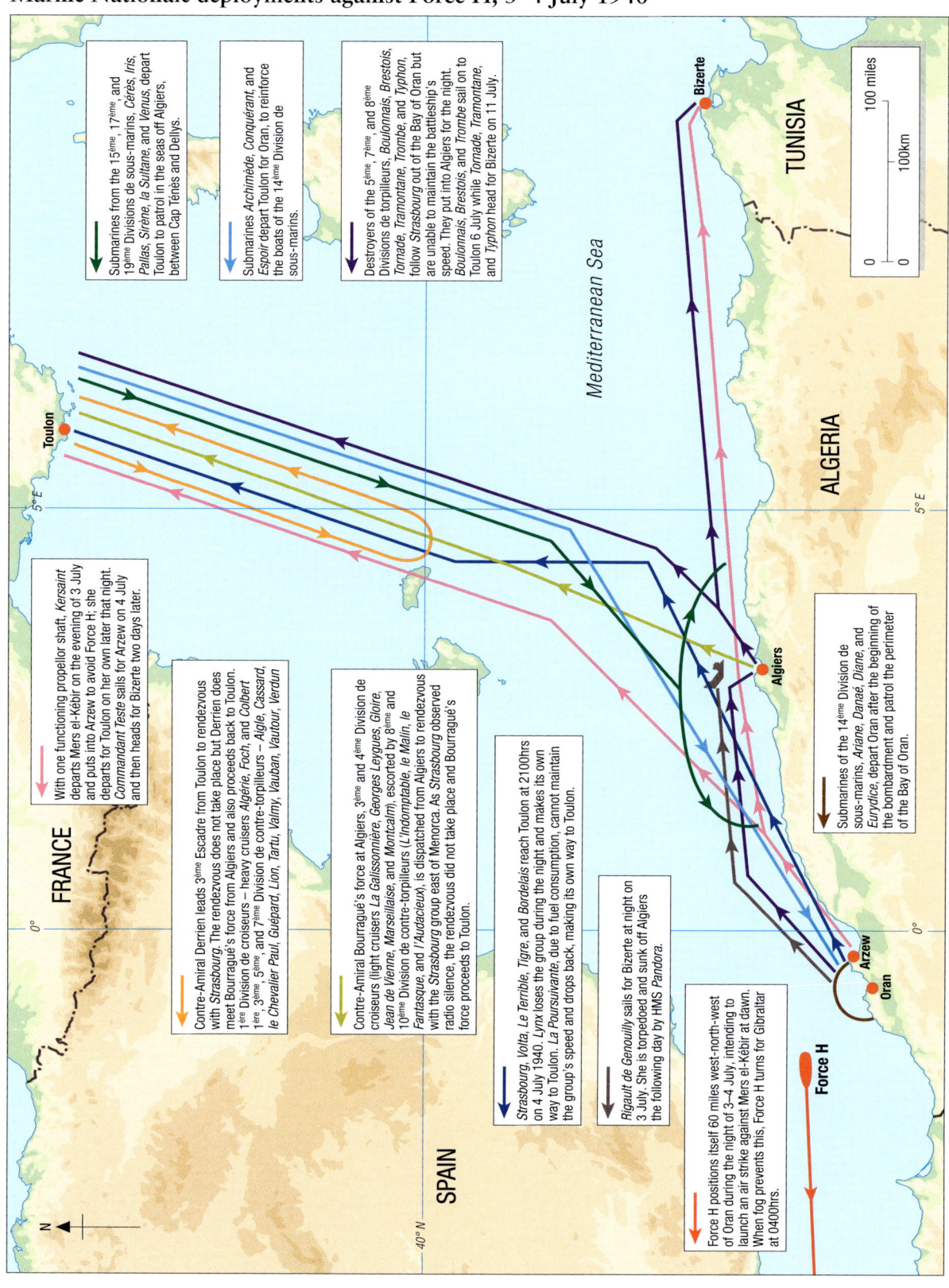

Submarines from the 15ème, 17ème, and 19ème Divisions de sous-marins, *Céres, Iris, Pallas, Sirène, la Sultane,* and *Venus,* depart Toulon to patrol in the seas off Algiers, between Cap Ténès and Dellys.

Submarines *Archimède, Conquérant,* and *Espoir* depart Toulon for Oran, to reinforce the boats of the 14ème Division de sous-marins.

Destroyers of the 5ème, 7ème, and 8ème Divisions de torpilleurs, *Boulonnais, Brestois, Tornade, Tramontane, Trombe,* and *Typhon,* follow *Strasbourg* out of the Bay of Oran but are unable to maintain the battleship's speed. They put into Algiers for the night. *Boulonnais, Brestois,* and *Trombe* sail on to Toulon 6 July while *Tornade, Tramontane,* and *Typhon* head for Bizerte on 11 July.

With one functioning propellor shaft, *Kersaint* departs Mers el-Kébir on the evening of 3 July and puts into Arzew to avoid Force H; she departs for Toulon on her own later that night. *Commandant Teste* sails for Arzew on 4 July and then heads for Bizerte two days later.

Contre-Amiral Derrien leads 3ème Escadre from Toulon to rendezvous with *Strasbourg*. The rendezvous does not take place but Derrien does meet Bourragué's force from Algiers and also proceeds back to Toulon. 1ère Division de croiseurs – heavy cruisers *Algérie, Foch,* and *Colbert* 1ère, 3ème, 5ème, and 7ème Division de contre-torpilleurs – *Aigle, Cassard, le Chevalier Paul, Guépard, Lion, Tartu, Valmy, Vauban, Vautour, Verdun*

Contre-Amiral Bourragué's force at Algiers, 3ème and 4ème Division de croiseurs (light cruisers *La Galissonnière, Georges Leygues, Gloire, Jean de Vienne, Marseillaise,* and *Montcalm*), escorted by 8ème and 10ème Division de contre-torpilleurs (*L'Indomptable, le Malin, le Fantasque,* and *l'Audacieux*), is dispatched from Algiers to rendezvous with the *Strasbourg* group east of Menorca. As *Strasbourg* observed radio silence, the rendezvous did not take place and Bourragué's force proceeds to Toulon.

Strasbourg, Volta, Le Terrible, Tigre, and *Bordelais* reach Toulon at 2100hrs on 4 July 1940. *Lynx* loses the group during the night and makes its own way to Toulon. *La Poursuivante,* due to fuel consumption, cannot maintain the group's speed and drops back, making its own way to Toulon.

Rigault de Genouilly sails for Bizerte at night on 3 July. She is torpedoed and sunk off Algiers the following day by HMS *Pandora.*

Submarines of the 14ème Division de sous-marins, *Ariane, Danaé, Diane,* and *Eurydice,* depart Oran after the beginning of the bombardment and patrol the perimeter of the Bay of Oran.

Force H positions itself 60 miles west-north-west of Oran during the night of 3–4 July, intending to launch an air strike against Mers el-Kébir at dawn. When fog prevents this, Force H turns for Gibraltar at 0400hrs.

TUNISIA

Bizerte

Mediterranean Sea

ALGERIA

5° E

5° E

Algiers

FRANCE

Toulon

0°

0°

SPAIN

40° N

Arzew

Oran

Force H

N

100 miles

100km

74

Gensoul could not put to sea in either of his remaining battleships, Darlan instructed Amiral Estéva at Bizerte to assume command over the increasing number of Marine Nationale deployments in the western Mediterranean. He then ordered Amiral Bourragué's two divisions of light cruisers from Algiers to rendezvous with *Strasbourg* and its consorts just east of the island of Minorca and then to pursue and engage Force H. Darlan had already authorized the departure of Amiral Derrien's 3ème Escadre from Toulon at 2000hrs to back up Collinet's and Bourragué's forces against Force H. Darlan's furious dispatch of units around the western Mediterranean on the afternoon and evening of 3 July proved to be the largest French naval deployment of World War II – ironically at a time when all of the vessels involved were supposed to have been demobilized under the terms of the Armistice of Rethondes.

Fortunately for Force H, Bourragué's cruisers were unable to locate *Strasbourg* during the night as Collinet maintained radio silence. As these French forces steamed their separate ways that night, Darlan was summoned to a meeting of ministers at Pétain's office in Vichy in the early morning hours. There, Darlan attempted to give a calm overview of his deployments the previous evening but was visibly shaking with rage and burst into a tirade about how he 'had been betrayed by his brothers in arms'. Paul Baudouin, Pétain's Ministre des Affaires étrangères (Minister of Foreign Affairs) who witnessed Darlan come unhinged, later wrote that the admiral looked as 'an ulcerated man, who above all seeks swift revenge'. Unwilling to risk all-out war with the British or to risk the fleet, which had become all too important of a bargaining piece with the Axis, Pétain instructed Darlan to rescind his 2030hrs order of the previous evening. At 0327hrs, a message from the Amirauté was sent to all surface vessels at sea in the western Mediterranean, ordering them to proceed to Toulon. At 2100hrs on the evening of 4 July, *Strasbourg* at last entered Toulon harbour to a hero's welcome, its arrival announced by the cheers of crews and whistles of ships. Collinet was promoted to contre-amiral the following month for his actions.

Darlan chafed at having to abandon the pursuit of Force H but followed the orders issued by Pétain. Another attack by the Royal Navy that day drove him into taking further independent action, however. That afternoon, HMS *Pandora*, one of the British submarines tasked with patrolling the exits to Oran and Algiers harbours the day before, was still on patrol off Algiers when at 1358hrs it spotted what appeared to be a French cruiser approaching from the west. It was actually the colonial sloop *Rigault de Genouilly*, which had engaged Somerville's battleships and cruisers the day before; it had left Oran at 2330hrs on 3 July and was bound for Bizerte in Tunisia. *Pandora*'s commander was still under Admiralty orders to fire on any French warship and at 1407hrs, after closing to a distance of 3,500m, launched four torpedoes at the sloop. Two struck the small vessel and, at 1522hrs, while sinking by the stern, *Rigault de Genouilly* was rocked by an explosion that broke the ship in two; 12 of its crew perished in the attack. When he learned of *Rigault de Genouilly*'s sinking, Darlan ordered the Aéronavale to immediately carry out retaliatory airstrikes against Gibraltar – without

A flight of Lioré et Olivier LeO H-257 bis twin-engine floatplanes, similar to those of Aéronavale Escadrille B-1 based at Port-Lyautey in Morocco, which made one of Darlan's 'vengeance' raids against Gibraltar on the night of 4/5 July. (Author's collection)

Armée de l'Air and Aéronavale retaliatory operations, 5–10 July 1940

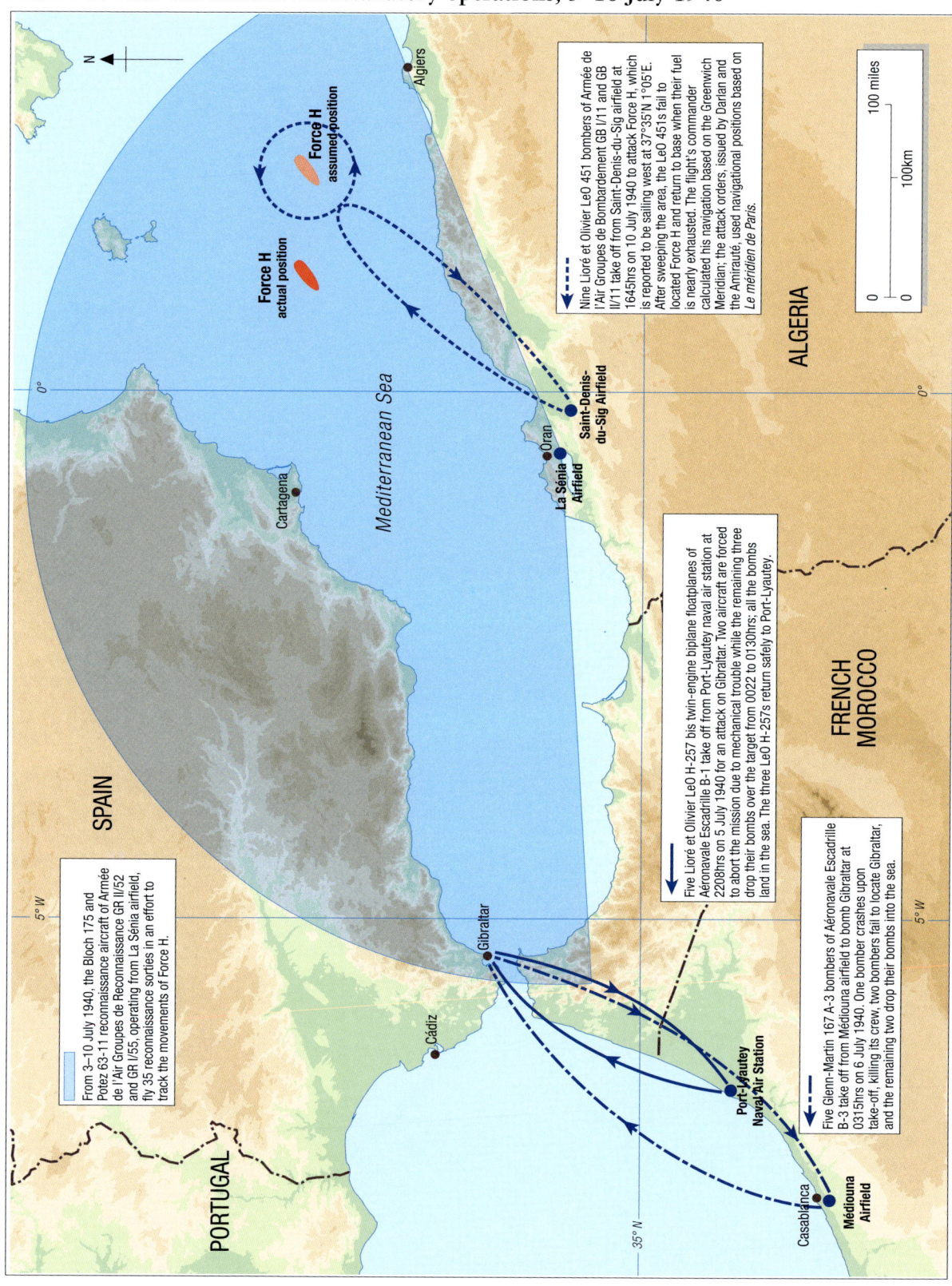

Nine Lioré et Olivier LeO 451 bombers of Armée de l'Air Groupes de Bombardement GB I/11 and GB II/11 take off from Saint-Denis-du-Sig airfield at 1645hrs on 10 July 1940 to attack Force H, which is reported to be sailing west at 37°35'N 1°05'E. After sweeping the area, the LeO 451s fail to located Force H and return to base when their fuel is nearly exhausted. The flight's commander calculated his navigation based on the Greenwich Meridian; the attack orders, issued by Darlan and the Amirauté, used navigational positions based on *Le méridien de Paris*.

Five Lioré et Olivier LeO H-257 bis twin-engine biplane floatplanes of Aéronavale Escadrille B-1 take off from Port-Lyautey naval air station at 2208hrs on 5 July 1940 for an attack on Gibraltar. Two aircraft are forced to abort the mission due to mechanical trouble while the remaining three drop their bombs over the target from 0022 to 0130hrs; all the bombs land in the sea. The three LeO H-257s return safely to Port-Lyautey.

Five Glenn-Martin 167 A-3 bombers of Aéronavale Escadrille B-3 take off from Médiouna airfield to bomb Gibraltar at 0315hrs on 6 July 1940. One bomber crashes upon take-off, killing its crew, two bombers fail to locate Gibraltar, and the remaining two drop their bombs into the sea.

From 3–10 July 1940, the Bloch 175 and Potez 63-11 reconnaissance aircraft of Armée de l'Air Groupes de Reconnaissance GR II/52 and GR I/55, operating from La Sénia airfield, fly 35 reconnaissance sorties in an effort to track the movements of Force H.

Force H assumed position

Force H actual position

Mediterranean Sea

Algiers

Saint-Denis-du-Sig Airfield

Oran

La Sénia Airfield

ALGERIA

SPAIN

Cartagena

Cádiz

Gibraltar

PORTUGAL

Port-Lyautey Naval Air Station

Casablanca

Médiouna Airfield

FRENCH MOROCCO

N

100 miles

100km

consulting Pétain or Weygand. This was another frenzied order as the squadrons of the Aéronavale, like those of the Armée de l'Air, had been in the process of demobilizing and disarming. That mattered little to Darlan, who wanted a swift show of force. By that evening, Escadrille B-1, based at Port-Lyautey in Morocco, managed to make five Lioré et Olivier LeO H-257 bis twin-engine floatplanes operational and arm them. These biplanes, with a maximum speed of only 150mph and a small bombload, would hardly make a formidable impression on the enemy, but in Darlan's mind they would have to suffice.

Glenn-Martin 167 A-3 medium bomber of Aéronavale Escadrille B-3. Like the Curtiss H-75, a number of these American-made bombers were purchased for the Armée de l'Air and Aéronavale due to French aviation production delays. Five Glenn-Martin 167s from Escadrille B-3 were also sent on a vengeance raid against Gibraltar in the early morning hours of 5 July, but one crashed upon take-off and only two of the others located the target. (Author's collection)

At 2208hrs, the biplanes slowly headed out over the Mediterranean towards Gibraltar. Shortly after take-off, however, two of the aircraft were forced to turn back with mechanical problems. Shortly after midnight on 5 July, as LeO H-257 B1-6 approached Gibraltar from the south-west, the unmistakable silhouette of the Rock loomed upon the dark horizon. The Rock was bathed at its base by the lights of the town and the naval base, which inexplicably had not yet been blacked out. Without pausing to question their good fortune, the crew of B1-6 approached the naval base at an altitude of 2,700m and dropped their bombs at 0022hrs. Content to have escaped from what could have been an extremely dangerous mission, the crew of B1-6 flew off, not realizing they had dropped their payload harmlessly in the waters of the harbour. When LeO H-257 B1-11 arrived overhead 12 minutes later, the lights around the Rock had been extinguished, the defenders alerted by the exploding bombs in the harbour. B1-11's bombs also landed in the sea. When LeO H-257 B1-2 approached at 0115hrs, however, the lights were back on, but this aircraft likewise failed to inflict any damage. The first aerial bombardment of Gibraltar in the war had been an ineffective exercise for both attacker and defender alike. A few hours later at Médiouna airfield just south of Casablanca, Escadrille B-3 answered Darlan's call to action and readied five Glenn-Martin 167 A-3 land-based bombers. Beginning at 0315hrs, the bombers began rolling down the runway. In the haste to carry out the mission, lights and beacons had not been set up around the airfield to assist with night operations and one of the aircraft crashed upon take-off, killing its entire crew. Of the four remaining Glenn-Martin 167s, two failed to locate Gibraltar in the darkness while the other two dropped their bombs into the sea. Darlan's desperate vengeance missions only demonstrated the poor state of French offensive air power. Pétain turned a blind eye to the whole affair.

OPERATION *LEVER* AND AFTERMATH

In Gibraltar, Somerville spent a restless night, but it was not because of the French air attacks. The admiral was sure he had earned the ire of Churchill and the Admiralty, writing to his wife: 'Afraid I shall get a colossal raspberry from the Admiralty for letting the Battlecruiser escape and not finishing off more French ships...' During the night of 3/4 July, Somerville had received a message from the Admiralty, ordering him to continue the pursuit of *Strasbourg* if it had been damaged in the earlier torpedo attack. He had already been sailing west for several hours by that time and could not confirm if *Strasbourg* had actually been damaged. In spite of what Somerville considered to have been a failed mission, late in the day on 4 July he received a complimentary message from the Admiralty, which also included praise from Churchill on the measure of success achieved. Dumbfounded, Somerville thanked them but admitted that he ordered a ceasefire at the earliest moment, personally repulsed by having to risk any more French lives than absolutely necessary. Unknown to Somerville, the Prime Minister had earlier that day delivered a speech before the House of Commons which outlined the actions taken on 3 July as well as his reasoning for them. In Churchill's words:

> A large proportion of the French fleet has therefore passed into our hands or has been put out of action or otherwise withheld from Germany by yesterday's events. The House will not expect me to say anything about the other French ships which are at large except that it is our inflexible resolve to do everything possible in order to prevent them from falling into German hands...
>
> The action we have already taken should, in itself, be sufficient to dispose once and for all of all the lies and rumours which have been so industriously spread in the United States and elsewhere by German propaganda and which you meet with here, fostered here at home by fifth column activities. These lies and rumours have suggested that we have had some intention of entering into negotiations with the German and Italian Governments. Any idea of that should be completely swept out of the way by the very drastic and grievous action we have felt ourselves compelled to take.

Churchill claimed that this drastic course of action was necessary to demonstrate British resolve to fight on to victory. Churchill's speech was met with thunderous applause from both sides of the political aisle and in the immediate aftermath he received almost universal praise in the British, and also American, media for the decisive action he took. This response was by no means predestined but it proved to be opportune and became the popular after-the-fact justification for the attack on Mers el-Kébir, propagated early on by Churchill in his post-war memoirs. Nevertheless, this assessment was not on Somerville's mind at the time. On the evening of 4 July, as Force H's vessels were refuelled and rearmed, he mulled over the 'hateful business' of the previous day, further telling his wife that he hated the idea of 'being regarded as the "unskilled butcher of Oran", or something like that'. His contemplation was interrupted by a message from the Admiralty, asking if he could confirm that the damage sustained by *Dunkerque* could keep it out of service for at least a year. The 'hateful business' was not yet concluded.

A bombastic public announcement made by Amiral Estéva on 4 July, in which he stated that *Dunkerque* had only received minimal damage and would soon be ready for action, had been relayed via British intelligence sources to Churchill, who in turn insisted that the Admiralty immediately address the issue. Somerville replied to the Admiralty that while *Dunkerque*

Aerial photograph of the disposition of Gensoul's remaining capital ships in Mers el-Kébir harbour on 4 July. *Dunkerque* (centre) is moored off the village of Saint André. Behind and to the left, the capsized *Bretagne*'s keel can be seen just in front of *Commandant Teste*. Behind and to the right is *Provence*, down by the stern and run aground off the villages of Roseville and Sainte-Clotilde. From the air, *Dunkerque* appeared relatively undamaged – particularly to Royal Navy observers. (Collection l'Association Amicale des Anciens Marins de Mers-el-Kébir et des Familles des Victimes)

had been observed on fire and damaged, he could not definitively assess the extent of the damage to the battleship. At 0308hrs on 5 July, Somerville received orders from the Admiralty to execute a second heavy bombardment against *Dunkerque*, codenamed Operation *Lever* and scheduled for the morning of 6 July. Churchill, still fixated on the balance of capital ships between the Royal Navy and the Axis, wanted *Dunkerque* definitively put out of action, and had convinced the War Cabinet of the necessity of a second attack. As originally drawn up by the Admiralty, the bombardment would be undertaken by *Hood* and *Valiant*, covered by *Ark Royal*, *Arethusa*, *Enterprise*, and nine destroyers; *Resolution* would be left behind due to its slower speed.

The slightly reduced Force H would depart Gibraltar on the evening of 5 June and make a feint to the west, confusing any Vichy submarines or reconnaissance aircraft that might be on patrol, and then turn eastward after dark. When 130km west of Oran, *Ark Royal*, *Enterprise*, and three destroyers would be detached to operate outside of immediate Vichy air cover, while the remainder of Force H would proceed to a point 7km north of Oran by 0900hrs, zero-hour for the attack. At 0830hrs, *Valiant* would launch its spotter aircraft to ascertain the exact positions of the warships in Mers el-Kébir harbour. At 0845hrs, Skuas, having earlier flown off from *Ark Royal* and armed with bombs, would arrive over the harbour and dive-bomb the 240mm coastal batteries at Cap Canastel and the 194mm batteries at Santon. At zero-hour, *Hood* and *Valiant* would target *Dunkerque* while *Arethusa* and the destroyers were left to engage the coastal batteries if necessary. Despite the heavy French fighter presence on 3 July, and the fact that the Armée de l'Air bomber squadrons had had three days to make their aircraft combat-ready, the Admiralty made little provision for the event of French air attack on Force H. Realizing that another bombardment by his battleships would result in further extensive French casualties and collateral damage on the nearby village of Saint André, Somerville asked the Admiralty if he could again attempt negotiations with Gensoul for peaceful demolition of *Dunkerque*, or if he could launch an aerial torpedo attack against the battleship. According to reconnaissance reports, *Dunkerque*'s present position in the harbour allowed for aerial torpedoes to be successfully deployed and Somerville reasoned that this method of attack would result in fewer French casualties, as Gensoul had likely evacuated his crews from the damaged warships. At 0224hrs on 6 July, as Force H steamed eastward, the Admiralty agreed to Somerville's request for an aerial torpedo attack. The time for zero-hour was amended for first light.

At 0515hrs in the predawn darkness, Lieutenant Commander Hodgkinson again led six torpedo-armed Swordfish of 820 Squadron off *Ark Royal*'s flight deck. With *Strasbourg* having escaped 820 Squadron's torpedo attacks three days earlier, some of Hodgkinson's crews must have been keen on success in this second mission. Hodgkinson led his flight on an eastward course at 2,100m, keeping 24km off the coast and outside of visual range from the harbour. Once the sun began to rise, Hodgkinson intended to descend in an arc to starboard around the perimeter of the Bay of Oran and, with the bright dawn sun masking his flight's movements, approach *Dunkerque* from the north-east, hopefully having maintained the element of surprise. At 0545hrs, a sub-flight of three torpedo-armed Swordfish from 810 Squadron, commanded by Captain Alan Newson, took off from *Ark Royal*, followed

Swordfish torpedo bombers, preparing to take off from *Ark Royal*. With the location of *Dunkerque* having changed, Somerville convinced the Admiralty to allow him to make a more effective torpedo attack to definitively disable the battleship in the follow-up Operation *Lever*, rather than another gunnery bombardment. (Daily Mirror/Mirrorpix via Getty Images)

immediately by two sections of three Skuas each from 803 Squadron, Blue Section led by Lieutenant J. Christian and Red Section led by Lieutenant D. Gibson. Lastly, at 0620hrs, another sub-flight of three Swordfish, led by Lieutenant D. Godfrey-Faussett from 810 Squadron, lifted off. The Skuas from 803 Squadron were to fly cover for the sub-flights from 810 Squadron, which were to complete the destruction of *Dunkerque* if the earlier attack by 820 Squadron had failed to do so.

As the first wave of Swordfish made their way towards Mers el-Kébir, all was relatively quiet in the harbour. Only skeleton crews, mostly maintenance teams, remained aboard *Dunkerque* and *Provence*; most of the able-bodied had been transferred to ocean liners in Oran while the wounded were housed in the hospital in Saint André. The fires aboard *Dunkerque* had finally been extinguished on 5 July, but it otherwise had been a sombre day; nearly 400 French sailors, victims of the 3 July bombardment, were laid to rest in the Aïn El Turk Cemetery in a solemn ceremony led by Amiral Gensoul. Thus, on the morning of 6 July, *Dunkerque*'s caretaker crew was fast asleep, exhausted from the trying events of the previous days. The anti-aircraft batteries aboard were no longer manned on Gensoul's orders; the admiral wanted the battleship to appear abandoned to British reconnaissance aircraft, which had continued to overfly the harbour, and power still had not been restored to her 138mm secondary turrets. *Dunkerque* was also immobile; the forward 30m of her bow had been run aground on 3 July in an effort to stem flooding caused by the shell hits along her hull. She was a sitting duck for what was to come.

Capitaine de Vaisseau Henri Seguin, *Dunkerque*'s commander, had not spent a restful night, however. He was bothered by an overflight made by a British flying boat the evening before. A similar flight had been made the evening before the attack on 3 July. As a precautionary measure, he had additional crew removed from the battleship that night and had three patrol boats – *Terre-Neuve*, *Sétoise*, and *Grouin de Cou* – moored alongside her in the event the remainder of the crew had to be evacuated during an attack. His suspicions turned out to be well justified. At 0605hrs, he received a message from lookouts stationed on the Habibas Islands, roughly 40km directly west of Mers el-Kébir: formation of aircraft at high altitude, proceeding east – the British were back. Seguin ran below and ordered the 330mm magazines to be flooded. He then ordered the patrol boats moored alongside *Dunkerque* to cast off and to get away from the battleship. They would be unable to get underway for half an hour, however, as their boilers needed to raise steam.

At 0625hrs, lookouts spotted low-flying aircraft approaching from the north. At an altitude of only 15m, Hodgkinson flew over the quay and over the damaged *Mogador*, which had been moored at the western end of the pier under Fort de Mers el-Kébir. At low speed, Hodgkinson's Swordfish slipped its torpedo into the water and banked away, followed by the other aircraft in the flight. Hodgkinson could not believe his good fortune; his flight appeared to make good torpedo runs, reporting that five out of the six torpedoes hit, and *Dunkerque* put up no anti-aircraft fire. Unfortunately for the Swordfish crews, the attack had not been a success. Five of the torpedoes had porpoised upon landing in the water, sending them off course and away from *Dunkerque*. One torpedo struck the *Terre-Neuve*, moored on *Dunkerque*'s starboard side under her 330mm turrets, but failed to explode. The torpedo did penetrate *Terre-Neuve*'s starboard side, however, and she began to slowly sink.

As Hodgkinson's flight headed off to the west, Newson's sub-flight from 810 Squadron arrived north of Oran and made a similar approach out of the sun from the east. Newson's sub-flight was greeted with heavy anti-aircraft fire from shore batteries on this occasion, the defenders having now had time to rally. The Swordfish took evasive manoeuvres during their approach over the Bay of Oran, dodging flak bursts and machine-gun fire, finally making their torpedo runs at 0650hrs over the far western end of the quay. Newson's rear gunner, seeing French sailors running to man an anti-aircraft gun on the quay as the aircraft approached, managed surprisingly accurate fire which drove the defenders off. Newson's pilot was unable to release his aircraft's torpedo and banked away, but the other two Swordfish dropped theirs with two hits reported. A column of water shot up along *Dunkerque*'s starboard side as Newson's sub-flight banked to port and made their way out to sea.

One torpedo did strike a target, but it was not *Dunkerque*. It struck the sinking *Terre-Neuve* and exploded, splitting the patrol boat in two. Most of *Dunkerque*'s crew had by now come out on deck to observe the action and to evacuate, and a number of sailors had rushed over to where *Terre-Neuve* had been moored, assisting survivors from the stricken patrol boat. Their act of mercy would prove to have tragic consequences, however. Shortly before 0700hrs, as 810 Squadron's sub-flight hugged the headland to the west of Mers el-Kébir to avoid anti-aircraft fire, Newson reported a large explosion in the harbour that rocked his aircraft; he assumed that one of the torpedo hits had detonated *Dunkerque*'s magazines. The explosion had actually come from the wreck of the little *Terre-Neuve*, which had been carrying 44 depth charges that morning, some of which were primed. As they sank with the boat, the water pressure caused the primed depth charges to explode, hence the delay between the torpedo strike and the large explosion. A total of 14 depth charges, equalling 1,400kg of TNT, went off, wrenching the starboard side of *Dunkerque*'s hull and breaking apart a portion of the main armoured belt. A large hole was torn open beneath turret no. 2, sending water pouring in, and causing the battleship to settle further into the harbour bottom. Most tragic of all, 30 officers and sailors were killed by the explosion and by shattered pieces of hull raining down on the deck. Had Capitaine

Dunkerque, moored off Saint André prior to the 6 July torpedo attack. The ill-fated gunboat *Terre-Neuve* is moored along her starboard side. (Collection l'Association Amicale des Anciens Marins de Mers-el-Kébir et des Familles des Victimes)

ROYAL NAVY AERIAL TORPEDO ATTACK ON *DUNKERQUE*, 0655HRS, 6 JULY 1940 (PP.82–83)

After learning from intelligence reports that *Dunkerque* had not been critically damaged in the 3 July bombardment, Churchill insisted upon another attack upon Mers el-Kébir by Force H to finish the battleship off. On the morning of 6 July 1940 in Operation *Lever*, three waves of Swordfish torpedo bombers from *Ark Royal* made torpedo runs against *Dunkerque*. The first wave, six Swordfish of 820 Squadron, led by Lieutenant Commander Hodgkinson, flew in from the east, out of the sun, and dropped to an altitude of 20ft before turning southward. The aircraft skimmed over the quay and alongside the damaged destroyer *Mogador* before slipping their torpedoes into the water against *Dunkerque*. Five of the torpedoes porpoised upon landing, bouncing up out of the water, which caused them to go off course; one torpedo struck the patrol boat *Terre-Neuve*, which was moored along *Dunkerque*'s starboard side, but failed to explode. At 0650hrs, a sub-flight of three Swordfish from 810 Squadron, led by Captain Alan Newson, began their approach towards *Dunkerque*, also coming out of the east, out of the sun. Newson's Swordfish had to take evasive action over the Bay of Oran, as by this time the

defender's anti-aircraft batteries were on full alert. After dropping to 20ft, Newson led his sub-flight over the quay, skimming over the pier and past *Mogador*. The anti-aircraft batteries aboard *Mogador*, and in Fort de Mers el-Kébir, fired at the Swordfish but had difficulty aiming as the aircraft were coming in at such a close distance. Newson's rear gunner, however, opened up on an anti-aircraft machine battery on the pier and sent its gunners diving for cover. Newson's pilot was unable to release the aircraft's torpedo, so the sub-flight leader was forced to bank away with their payload still attached. Newson's squadron mates, however, successfully released their torpedoes, one of which detonated against *Terre-Neuve*, splitting the gunboat in half. Several minutes later, some of the depth charges aboard the wreck of the gunboat exploded underwater, wrenching a large breach in *Dunkerque*'s starboard hull and causing *Terre-Neuve* to settle on the harbour bottom. Seen here, Captain Newson's Swordfish (**1**) roars past the damaged *Mogador* (**2**) and Fort de Mers el-Kébir (**3**) at low altitude, leading his sub-flight in their successful attack on *Dunkerque* (**4**).

(Right) Swordfish torpedo bomber releasing an aerial torpedo. (Left) Captain Alan Newson, whose sub-flight from 810 Squadron delivered the torpedo that broke *Terre-Neuve* in half and triggered the explosion of the depth charges. (Author's collection)

Seguin not flooded the 330mm magazines prior to the attacks, *Dunkerque* would have likely been completely destroyed. As it was, this new damage was significant enough to keep her from being operational for considerable time. Somerville's objective of rendering *Dunkerque* inoperable for at least a year had finally been achieved, but the battle was not yet over.

After the explosion, Godfrey-Faussett's sub-flight from 810 Squadron arrived on the scene and began its attack run. Coming in from the north-west, the three Swordfish flew low over Fort de Mers el-Kébir and then, proceeding over the town of Mers el-Kébir, turned to port and made their torpedo runs against *Dunkerque*'s port side, from the southern end of the harbour. Two torpedoes were reported to strike the already crippled *Dunkerque* but failed to explode. The third torpedo hit the tug *Estérel*, which three days earlier had valiantly assisted *Dunkerque* in getting underway during the bombardment. *Estérel* was on her way to assist in the evacuation of the battleship but instead was literally blown out of the water by the torpedo and sank. Following their torpedo runs, Godfrey-Faussett's aircraft banked to starboard and turned to the north to make their getaway. Their escape would be a bit more eventful than those of the previous Swordfish flights. After passing over the quay, they were attacked by two three-aircraft patrols of H-75 fighters of GC II/5, led by Capitaine Portalis, a veteran of the 3 July aerial actions.

Dramatic photograph showing the explosion of the depth charges aboard the sinking *Terre-Neuve*. *Dunkerque* is already beginning to list to starboard. (© *Tous droits réservés Ministère des armées - Mémoire des hommes*, Conservé au Musée national de la Marine, Inv. CE 2018.6.7)

Pilots of Groupe de Chasse II/5: Sous-Lieutenant Paul Marcel Hebrard (left, first row), Sous-Lieutenant Paul Boudier (right, first row), Capitaine Hubert Monraisse (left, second row), and Capitaine Gérard Portalis (right, fourth row) all engaged the Skuas of 803 Squadron during 818 Squadron's bombing attack against *Strasbourg* on the evening of 3 July. Portalis again fought 803 Squadron's Skuas during Operation *Lever* on the morning of 6 July. (Author's collection)

Portalis and his comrades scrambled at Saint-Denis-du-Sig airfield at 0635hrs, shortly after the British attack began, but up to this time had not come across any enemy aircraft. This attack on the Swordfish did not last long, however, because the French H-75s were then dived upon by the six Skuas of 803 Squadron. The three Skuas of Blue Section had been patrolling at 3,000m north-east of the harbour when they spotted the H-75s sweeping in on the Swordfish, while the Skuas of Red Section had been engaged in taking photographs over the harbour. As the Skuas dived in, a swirling melee began over the seas just to the north of the harbour.

Midshipman A. Griffith of Blue Section, piloting Skua L.2961, led the charge against the H-75s, targeting one flown by one of Portalis' wingmen, Chief Sergeant Gisclon. Griffith swept in from behind, firing at the starboard rear of Gisclon's fighter, which quickly broke away in a vertical loop. Soon, thanks to the H-75's superior speed and manoeuvrability, Gisclon was on the tail of Griffith. Other H-75s came in from behind and Griffith began a series of tight turns and spins to shake off his pursuers. The H-75s easily followed but Griffith noticed that none of the French pilots seemed to be aggressively attacking; they fired several machine-gun bursts but only from long range. After a half hour of twirling acrobatics, Griffith flew into a cloud bank and the H-75s did not pursue.

Meanwhile, Portalis alone engaged three Skuas for the first ten minutes of the battle, firing at one at long distance and then breaking away when the other two came around on his tail. Two of the Skuas eventually turned away and headed out to sea, while Portalis remained on the tail of the third. The Skua then went into a vertical climb and upon stalling, dived down to starboard and levelled out into a cloud bank at 600m over Oran harbour; Portalis did not pursue into the clouds. Griffith was the most aggressive of the British pilots and attempted to fight several H-75s, but always found himself easily outmanoeuvred. Almost every British pilot gave the same assessment after the battle: although the H-75s clearly outflew the slow and cumbersome Skuas, no French pilot pressed the attack, with most French fire seeming to be aimed wide.

Around 0730hrs, most of the Skuas retired, except for Blue Section Leader Christian, who remained on patrol over the retreating Swordfish for another 40 minutes; the H-75s did not attempt to engage him. In fact, Griffith, the last of the other five Skuas to depart, was followed by several H-75s for half an hour out to sea, almost as if he was being escorted off of property he had trespassed on. As Portalis and Gisclon turned back towards Saint-Denis-du-Sig, they spotted the low-flying Swordfish of Lieutenant Newson. Portalis dived in on the slow-moving biplane but when he pulled the trigger – nothing; he was out of ammunition. Gisclon then moved in and briefly fired until his ammunition was quickly spent. The Swordfish was damaged but still airworthy. Newson's rear-gunner went to return fire but damage to the machine-gun mount prevented him from doing so. All three aircraft, unable to fire, went their separate ways. *Ark Royal* recovered all the aircraft that participated in the raid on *Dunkerque* with no casualties among the flight crews. After that, Somerville ordered Force H to withdraw to the west, reaching Gibraltar that evening at 1830hrs.

The last move in the battles for Mers el-Kébir would be undertaken by the French, however. Beside himself with rage after yet another British attack, Darlan again demanded immediate reprisals on the Royal Navy. This time, Pétain and Weygand agreed that a show of force was necessary to deter future attacks, and Général Pennès was ordered to orchestrate an immediate aerial response against Force H from his North African Armée de l'Air bomber squadrons. Now three days after the initial attack at Mers el-Kébir, the various Groupes de Bombardement were still in a disorganized state; the primary problem was locating parts and ammunition, as much of this was still unaccounted for due to chaotic evacuation across the Mediterranean of crews, aircraft, and supplies in the days before the armistice. At the time, only GB I/11 and GB II/11, then based at Blida airfield outside Algiers, had enough operable aircraft to conduct a reasonable bombardment mission, and Pennès hastily ordered their immediate transfer to Oran. When the Lioré et Olivier LeO 451 medium bombers arrived at Saint-Denis-du-Sig airfield, they were instructed that they would be carrying out a bombardment at 1800hrs of Force H, now being shadowed by Armée de l'Air and Aéronavale reconnaissance aircraft. Lieutenant-Colonel Marcel Edouard Chopin, commander of Groupe de Bombardement 11, replied that this would be impossible as his aircraft still lacked essential navigational equipment and armament. To Darlan's chagrin, Force H slipped away unscathed again.

His anger continued to boil over as on 8 July the Royal Navy launched an aerial torpedo attack, independent from Operation *Catapult* and the follow-up Operation *Lever*, on the battleship *Richelieu* in Dakar. An opportunity to strike back at Force H presented itself on 10 July, however, when Somerville was again at sea in the western Mediterranean. Force H had left Gibraltar on 8 July to launch an air attack on Cagliari, Sardinia, on the following day, serving as a diversion from a convoy sailing from Alexandria to Malta; the air attack was subsequently cancelled, and Force H turned back for Gibraltar on the evening of 9 July. At 1115hrs on 10 July, a Bloch 175 reconnaissance aircraft from Groupe de Reconnaissance II/52 spotted Force H sailing to the west at 18 knots roughly 200km north-west of Algiers.

At 1515hrs, Lieutenant-Colonel Chopin was again ordered to attack and this time he managed to assemble nine operable and armed LeO 451s, six from GB I/11 and three from GB II/11. Take off was delayed, however, because the aircrafts' navigational charts had been left in Blida; a courier aircraft was rapidly dispatched to retrieve them. Finally, at 1645hrs, with the charts having been flown in, the nine LeO 451s, commanded by Capitaine Marc Hériard-Dubreuil, took off. In spite of clear skies, nothing was seen when the bombers reached Force H's estimated position. The bombers extended their search area but could find nothing, eventually having to drop their payloads in the sea and return to base at 2000hrs when their fuel ran low. As it turned out, Hériard-Dubreuil calculated his navigation based on the Greenwich Meridian; the attack orders, issued by Darlan and the Amirauté, used navigational positions based on *Le méridien de Paris*. It was a disappointing, and perhaps farcical, conclusion to what had been a disappointing and tragic series of events.

Lioré et Olivier LeO 451 medium bomber of the Armée de l'Air's Groupe de Bombardement I/11, photographed at Le Sénia airfield in 1941. In the last combat action of Operations *Catapult* and *Lever*, nine LeO 451s from GB I/11 and GB II/11 attempted to attack Force H in the western Mediterranean on 10 July but failed to locate the British force. (Author's collection

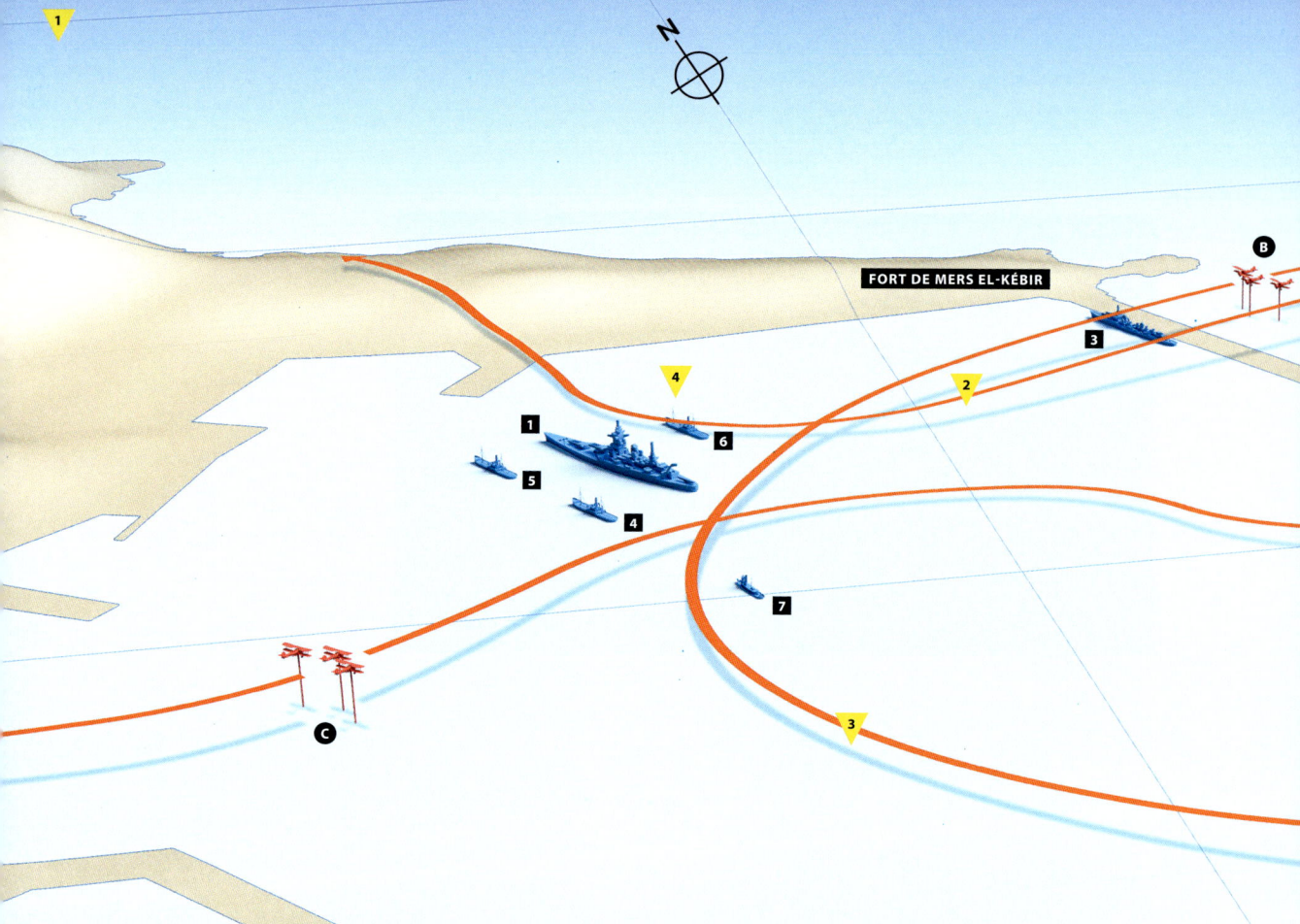

FORT DE MERS EL-KÉBIR

ROYAL NAVY AERIAL TORPEDO ATTACK ON *DUNKERQUE* IN MERS EL-KÉBIR HARBOUR, 0605–0730HRS, 6 JULY 1940

As the sun rose over Mers el-Kébir harbour in the early morning hours of 6 July 1940, twelve British Swordfish torpedo bombers, in three waves, made torpedo attacks against the battleship *Dunkerque*. Admiral Somerville had been ordered to finish off the damaged vessel by Churchill, who was desperate to sink at least one of the Marine Nationale's modern battleships after *Strasbourg*'s unexpected escape on the evening of 3 July. The attack would demonstrate the vulnerability of modern capital ships in port to aerial torpedo attack, even by obsolescent aircraft like the Swordfish – a strategy successfully employed again by the Royal Navy five months later at Taranto and also by the Imperial Japanese Navy a year and a half later at Pearl Harbor.

▼ EVENTS

1. 0605hrs. Six torpedo-armed Swordfish of 820 Squadron, led by Lieutenant Commander Hodgkinson and having taken off from *Ark Royal* at 0515hrs, are spotted flying eastward by French lookouts on the Habibas Islands. Upon receiving this report, Captain Seguin of *Dunkerque* orders the evacuation of his ship.

2. 0625–0630hrs. After turning and descending over the Bay of Oran, with the rising sun at their backs, Hodgkinson's Swordfish make their torpedo run. Five torpedoes go astray and one strikes the patrol boat *Terre-Neuve*, moored along *Dunkerque*'s starboard side, but fails to explode. *Terre-Neuve*, loaded with 44 depth charges – some of which are primed – begins to sink.

3. 0650hrs. Three torpedo-armed Swordfish from 810 Squadron, led by Captain Newson and having departed *Ark Royal* at 0545hrs, begin their torpedo run, coming in from the same direction as Hodgkinson's strike but taking evasive action up to the target due to anti-aircraft fire. One torpedo fails to drop, one misses, and the other hits *Terre-Neuve* and explodes, breaking the patrol boat in two.

4. 0655hrs. 14 depth charges in the wreck of *Terre-Neuve* explode, breaking open the starboard side of *Dunkerque*'s hull beneath turret no. 2. Water rushes into the breach and it settles further on the harbour bottom.

5. 0700hrs. Three torpedo-armed Swordfish from 810 Squadron, led by Lieutenant Godfrey-Faussett and having flown off *Ark Royal* at 0620hrs, sweep in from the north-west over Fort de Mers el-Kébir and then bank to port over the town of Mers el-Kébir to attack *Dunkerque* from its port side. Two torpedoes miss and the third strikes *Estérel*, sinking the tug.

6. 0700–0730hrs. Curtiss H-75 fighters from Groupe de Chasse II/5, after scrambling from Saint-Denis-du-Sig at 0635hrs, attempt to engage the retreating Swordfish north of Mers el-Kébir. They are pounced by Blackburn Skuas from 803 Squadron, which flew off *Ark Royal* after Newson's sub-flight. A swirling dogfight ensues for roughly half an hour. The French pilots, possessing overall superior fighters, do not press home their attacks and the British aircraft eventually withdraw northward. Neither side loses any aircraft.

6

A

5

INCOMPLETE
SECTION OF JETTY

BAY OF ORAN

FRENCH
1. *Dunkerque* (Dunkerque-class battleship)
2. *Provence* (Bretagne-class battleship)
3. *Mogador* (Mogador-class destroyer)
4. *Grouin de Cou* (World War I-era patrol boat)
5. *Sétoise* (World War I-era patrol boat)
6. *Terre-Neuve* (World War I-era patrol boat)
7. *Estérel* (harbour tug)

2

BRITISH
A. Hodgkinson's 820 Squadron flight (six Swordfish)
B. Newson's 810 Squadron sub-flight (three Swordfish)
C. Godfrey-Faussett's 810 Squadron sub-flight (three Swordfish)

ROSEVILLE

AFTERMATH

ANALYSIS AND CONCLUSION

The question of whether or not Operation *Catapult* was a success or failure is largely relative to several different perspectives of the time. If strictly determined by the operation's original objectives as given to Admiral Somerville, Operation *Catapult* could only be considered a partial tactical success at best. In terms of priority, *Dunkerque* received damage which kept it out of the war for over a year. After lengthy repairs, it finally was able to return to Toulon under its own power on 20 February 1942. *Strasbourg* escaped the bombardment and subsequent pursuit relatively undamaged and became the flagship of the Forces de haute mer (High Sea Force), a rump Marine Nationale permitted to Pétain's state by the Axis armistice commissions on 25 September 1940. *Bretagne* was a total loss, its wreck resting at the bottom of Mers el-Kébir harbour until broken up on site between 1952 and 1954. *Provence* was refloated already on 26 July 1940 and returned to Toulon in November 1940; it was repaired and back in service in early 1942, assigned to training duties.

Of the other warships attacked in Mers el-Kébir harbour, *Mogador* was made seaworthy and towed to Toulon in December 1940, but, due to wartime shortages, was never fully repaired. Outside of Mers el-Kébir, the warships of Amiral Godfroy's Force X were never taken over by the Royal Navy, but they did join the Free French movement in May 1943. Lastly, the warships seized in British ports proved to be of little value to the Royal Navy, as most were light auxiliary vessels. The few larger vessels were either too old for frontline use or required manpower which the Free French movement did not possess early in the war.

When counting up the number of French ships denied to Pétain's state or possibly Axis use, one destroyed modernized dreadnought battleship and only older or light auxiliary vessels seized did not amount to a significant gain for the Royal Navy. The most catastrophic result of Operation *Catapult* was that if the primary goal of the operation had been to keep French warships free from potential Axis seizure, it did the exact opposite. Most French warships in North African ports were transferred to Toulon in the days following Operation *Catapult*. What this meant was that the bulk of the Marine Nationale now sat within a day's drive for German panzers if Hitler decided he wished to seize the ships. In this light, Operation *Catapult* could be viewed as a strategic failure. And then there was the question of whether or not Vichy

France, the colloquial name used for Pétain's state by the Allies after Operation *Catapult*, would go to war with Great Britain. Ultimately, it did not in a strict sense, but that was not known for certain in the aftermath of the attacks. These concerns weighed heavily in the immediate assessments of Operation *Catapult* by Admiral Somerville, Admiral Cunningham, and other senior officers within the Royal Navy.

To Churchill, Operation *Catapult* was nothing short of an unqualified success; or at least, this is what he later wrote. As mentioned previously, already on 4 July 1940 Churchill was claiming that the attack at Mers el-Kébir was necessary to demonstrate British resolve to fight on until final victory. At the time, with victory far from certain and German preparations for *Unternehmen Seelöwe*, the planned invasion of Great Britain, just beginning, this could be viewed as having been a shot in the dark. After the war, in his second volume of his *The Second World War*, Churchill wrote of the attack on Mers el-Kébir:

Photograph of the extensive damage to *Dunkerque*'s starboard hull beneath turret no. 2 where *Terre-Neuve*'s depth charges exploded. The masts of the sunken gunboat are protruding from the water. (Collection l'Association Amicale des Anciens Marins de Mers-el-Kébir et des Familles des Victimes)

> The elimination of the French Navy as an important factor almost at a single stroke by violent action produced a profound impression in every country. Here was this Britain which so many had counted down and out, which strangers had supposed to be quivering on the brink of surrender to the might power arrayed against her, striking ruthlessly at her dearest friends of yesterday and securing for a while to herself the undisputed command of the sea. It was made plain that the British War Cabinet feared nothing and would stop at nothing. This was true…
>
> Immense relief spread through the high Government circles in the United States. The Atlantic Ocean seemed to regain its sheltering power, and a long vista of time opened out for the necessary preparations for the safety of the great Republic.

The actual damage done at Mers el-Kébir proved the first line above as false, but time would prove Churchill's assertion of British resolve as true. Fortunately for Churchill, President Franklin D. Roosevelt of the United States was personally impressed enough by the determined ruthlessness demonstrated by the British at Mers el-Kébir that it influenced him to agree on 30 August 1940 to the transfer of 50 United States Navy destroyers to the Royal Navy in exchange for American basing rights in British overseas territories. This agreement marked the beginning of the wartime Anglo-American partnership that would eventually lead to full alliance. The idea that Operation *Catapult* was designed to influence domestic and particularly foreign opinion on Great Britain's resolve to continue the war, as argued after the fact by Churchill, has become the standard explanation for such a drastic military operation in popular histories of World War II, and even in some academic studies. It has become part of the 'Finest Hour' narrative in heroic retellings of

The human cost of Operation *Catapult*; Amiral Gensoul presides over a funeral ceremony for fallen French officers and seamen at the Aïn El Turk Cemetery outside of Oran. (Keystone-France via Getty Images)

the dire months in 1940, from Dunkirk through the Battle of Britain, when Great Britain faced the German juggernaut against overwhelming odds.

For Darlan, Operation *Catapult* was a double-edged sword. Beyond *Dunkerque* being disabled and *Bretagne* lost, there was the tragic loss of skilled officers and sailors in both Operations *Catapult* and *Lever* – 1,248 dead and over 300 wounded (deaths from the ships' complements: *Bretagne* – 1,012; *Dunkerque* – 186; *Mogador* – 38; *Strasbourg* – 5; *Provence* – 3; from the Oran coastal defences – 4). Photographs taken of the casualties aboard the ships and the graves of the fallen confirmed Darlan's long-held belief in British perfidy. On the other hand, Darlan also viewed Operation *Catapult* as a blessing in disguise for both himself and the Marine Nationale in the difficult circumstances which Vichy France found itself in. After the attacks, Darlan found his position as commander of the Marine Nationale all the more secure, and his prestige had increased in both the eyes of Pétain and those of the Axis leadership. The rigorous defence put up by the Marine Nationale, Armée de l'Air, and Aéronavale during the attacks had impressed the Germans enough to allow the Vichy regime to reactivate the French armed services, albeit to a limited extent. Darlan propagated the idea that in the midst of Operation *Catapult*, the Marine Nationale, with himself at the helm, had won back French agency, against the backdrop of France's recent surrender to Germany. For a time, Darlan was touted as a French saviour by many of his loyal crews and by the Vichy leadership. In the coming months, Darlan would become the most influential member of the Vichy government, second only to Pétain, and was named the *maréchal*'s successor. While this was a temporary personal gain for Darlan, and while he argued his actions asserted an independent course of French action – thus preserving French *honneur* – it would forever associate him with the collaborationist actions of the Vichy regime – particularly in the histories of the conflict written by the victors.

If there was a clear beneficiary from the events of Operation *Catapult*, it was the Axis. In a meeting with Count Galeazzo Ciano, Italy's Foreign Minister, on 7 July 1940, Hitler was reported to express his satisfaction over the course of events regarding the Marine Nationale. From an official summary of Hitler's conversation with Ciano:

> Thus, for example, it had been very fortunate that the *Duce* and he (the *Führer*) had not insisted on the surrender of the French fleet. One would never get the French fleet that way. But now, by this intelligent handling of the fleet question, England and France had been made mutual enemies. This eased the situation considerably, in particular for Italy, and improved the situation in the western Mediterranean as well as the position of the Axis Powers with respect to Franco.
>
> The Führer expressed his satisfaction over the fact that the Italian armistice terms had been so formulated as to contribute to the present favourable situation as to France. The fact that even though there was a French sham government in London, there was on French territory a French government under Pétain, to which the French colonies had also adhered, was doubtless a great advantage for Italy and Germany.

The Anglo-Vichy conflict, which began during Operation *Catapult*, continued for another two years, with the French colonial empire in North and West Africa providing a convenient buffer from Allied attack until Operation *Torch* in November 1942. Furthermore, British and Allied resources were diverted into several campaigns in Africa and Asia in subduing perceived Axis threats in coordination with Vichy forces.

Ironically, two years after Operation *Catapult*, both Churchill and Darlan would be to some extent vindicated for their claims made during the French collapse in June 1940. In spite of his solemn promise to allow the French to keep the vessels of the Marine Nationale in the terms of the Armistice of Rethondes, Hitler eventually succumbed to the temptation of modern French vessels for potential Axis use. On 27 November 1942, in the midst of the Axis occupation of the Vichy state, Hitler launched *Unternehmen Lila*, the capture of the port of Toulon and the seizure of the Marine Nationale vessels there. This action proved Churchill correct – Hitler's promises were worth less than the paper upon which they were written. Nevertheless, *Unternehmen Lila* would prove Darlan to be true in his claim that the Marine Nationale would never allow its vessels to fall into German hands. While German panzers swept through the Toulon citadel, Amiral Jean de Laborde, who had succeeded Darlan as commander of the Vichy Forces de Haute Mer, gave the long-anticipated 'scuttle' order in the event of enemy capture, which Darlan had established back in June 1940. There were 77 French vessels destroyed – including Mers el-Kébir veterans *Dunkerque*, *Strasbourg*, *Provence*, *Commandant Teste*, *Mogador*, *Lynx*, *Tigre*, and *Kersaint* – over the course of the day, denying the Germans and Italians the use of any significant warships of the Marine Nationale. Of further irony was the fact that Churchill and Darlan were forced to work together for several weeks at the end of 1942. On 10 November 1942 at the outset of Operation *Torch*, the Allied invasion of North Africa, Darlan, who was in North Africa, offered his services to Lieutenant General Dwight D. Eisenhower, Supreme Commander Allied Expeditionary Force, in arranging the ceasefire of all French armed forces there. In return, Darlan demanded to be made Commandement en chef français civil et militaire (High Commissioner of France in Africa), the new civil and military commander of all French forces in Africa. In order to expedite the Allied campaign, Eisenhower agreed and was supported in his decision by both Roosevelt and Churchill. When faced with domestic and foreign criticism, particularly from the Free French movement, of Darlan's new appointment in North Africa, Churchill wrote to Eisenhower: 'Anything for the battle, but the politics will have to be sorted out later on.' It was a statement indicative of Churchill's stubborn pursuit of victory, at any cost. On 24 December 1942, Darlan was assassinated in a random event by, of all parties, a French monarchist. It was a confused end to what was, perhaps euphemistically, a confused wartime career.

Darlan, as Vice-président du Conseil of the Vichy government, meeting with Hitler at Berchtesgaden on 12 May 1941. While Darlan staunchly believed he advocated and acted for independent French agency following the Armistice of Rethondes (and was certainly not pro-German), his prominent role in Pétain's government would forever associate him with Vichy collaborationist efforts. (Keystone-France via Getty Images)

Panzer IV of the 7.Panzer-Division parked on a pier next to the scuttled *Strasbourg* during the German capture of Toulon on 27 November 1942. In the end, both Churchill and Darlan were proven correct: Hitler could not be trusted, and no major French warship fell into German hands. (Author's collection)

BIBLIOGRAPHY

PRIMARY SOURCES

The National Archives (UK)

    Admiralty Record ADM 199-391: Force 'H' War Diaries

    Admiralty Record ADM 199-392: Force 'H' War Diaries

    Admiralty Record ADM 234-317: Battle Summaries

    Admiralty Record ADM 53/111437: Ship's Log

SECONDARY SOURCES

Antier, Jean-Jacques. *L'Aventure héroïque des sous-mariniers Français 1939–1945*. Paris: Editions maritimes & d'outre-mer, 1984.

Auphan, Paul and Mordal, Jacques. *The French Navy in World War II*. Annapolis: United States Naval Institute, 1959.

Beltjens, François. *Mers El-Kébir 3 Juillet 1940. Exécution ou bataille perdue*. Paris: Godefroy de Bouillon, 2000.

Böhme, Hermann. *Entstehung und Grundlagen des Waffenstillstandes von 1940*. Stuttgart: Deutsche Verlags-Anstalt, 1966.

Boutron, Jean. *De Mers el-Kébir à Londres*. Paris: Plon, 1980.

Brown, David. *The Road to Oran: Anglo-French Naval Relations September 1939–July 1940*. London: Taylor & Francis Ltd, 2001.

Churchill, Winston S. *Speech by The Prime Minister Mr. Winston Churchill On the Taking of the French Fleet, Delivered in the House of Commons, July 4, 1940*. New York: The British Library of Information, 1940.

Churchill, Winston S. *The Second World War. Volume II: Their Finest Hour*. Boston: Houghton Mifflin Harcourt, 1948.

Churchill, Winston S. *The Second World War. Volume IV: The Hinge of Fate*. Boston: Houghton Mifflin Harcourt, 1950.

Coutau-Bégarie, Hervé and Huan, Claude. *Darlan*. Paris: Fayard, 1989.

Davis, Richard. *Anglo-French Relations Before the Second World War: Appeasement and Crisis*. Basingstoke, Hampshire: Palgrave, 2001.

Discepoli, Bénédicte. *Direction des Constructions Navales Ruelle Artillerie de Marine: Plans de Canons et de Navires, 1866–1951*. Châtellerault: Ministere de la Defense, 2009.

Draper, Alfred. *Operation Fish: The Race to Save Europe's Wealth 1939–1945*. London: Cassell, 1979.

Ehrengardt, C.J. and Shores, Christopher F. *L'aviation de Vichy au combat*. Paris: Lavauzelle, 1985.

Frémont, Marcel. *La déraison d'Etat: Mers El-Kébir, 1940*. Paris: Janus, 1997.

Godfroy, René Émile. *L'Aventure de la Force X: escadre française de la Méditerranée orientale, à Alexandrie, 1940–1943*. Paris: Plon, 1953.

Greene, Jack and Massignani, Alessandro. *The Naval War in the Mediterranean 1940–1943*. London: Chatham Publishing, 1998.

Jackson, Julian. *France: The Dark Years, 1940–1944*. Oxford: Oxford University Press, 2001.

Jordan, John and Caresse, Philippe. *French Battleships of World War One*. Annapolis: Naval Institute Press, 2017.

Jordan, John and Dumas, Robert. *French Battleships: 1922–1956*. Barnsley: Seaforth Publishing, 2014.

Kammerer, Albert. *La passion de la flotte française, de Mers el-Kébir à Toulon*. Paris: Fayard, 1951.

Lasterle, Philippe. 'Could Admiral Gensoul Have Averted the Tragedy of Mers el-Kébir?' *The Journal of Military History*, Vol. 67, No. 3 (2003), pp. 835–44.

Lormier, Dominique. *Mers el-Kébir Juillet 1940*. Paris: Calmann-Lévy, 2007.

Marder, Arthur J. *From the Dardanelles to Oran: Studies of the Royal Navy in War and Peace, 1915–1940*. London: Oxford University Press, 1974.

Martin, Jacqueline, and Martin, Paul. *Ils étaient là: l'armée de l'air, septembre 39–juin 40*. Fleurance: Aéro éd., 2001.

Masson, Philippe. *La marine française et la guerre, 1939–1945*. Paris: Tallandier, 2000.

Melka, Robert L. 'Darlan Between Britain and Germany 1940–41.' *Journal of Contemporary History*, Vol. 8, No. 2 (Apr. 1973), pp. 57–80.

Melton, George E. *From Versailles to Mers el-Kébir: The Promise of Anglo-French Naval Cooperation, 1919–1940*. Annapolis: Naval Institute Press, 2015.

Michel, Henri. *François Darlan*. Paris: Hachette, 1993.

Olch, Isaiah. 'The Jean Bart's Escape to Safety.' *Proceedings, U.S. Naval Institute*, Vol. 82, No. 10 (Oct. 1956).

Parker, R. A. C. *Churchill and Appeasement*. London: Macmillan, 2000.

Persyn, Lionel. *Les Curtiss H-75 de l'Armée de l'Air: Histoire de l'Aviation Nr. 22*. Le Vigen: Lela Presse, 2008.

Roskill, Stephen Wentworth. *Churchill and the Admirals*. New York: William Morrow and Company, Inc., 1978.

Rimbaud, Christiane. *L'affaire du Massilia: Été 1940*. Paris: Seuil, 1984.

Saffroy, Frédéric. *Le Bouclier de Neptune: La politique de défense des bases françaises en Méditerranée (1912–1931)*. Rennes: Presses universitaires de Rennes, 2015.

Salerno, Reynolds M. 'The French Navy and the Appeasement of Italy, 1937–9.' *The English Historical Review*, Vol. 112, No. 445 (Feb. 1997), pp. 66–104.

Sweet, Paul R. (ed.), et al. *Documents on German Foreign Policy, 1918–1945. Series D, Volume X, The War Years, June 23–August 31, 1940*. Washington DC: United States Government Printing Office, 1957.

Thomas, Martin. 'At the Heart of Things? French Imperial Defense Planning in the Late 1930s.' *French Historical Studies*, Vol. 21, No. 2 (Spring 1998), pp. 325–61.

Young, Robert J. 'French Military Intelligence and the Franco-Italian Alliance, 1933–1939.' *The Historical Journal*, Vol. 28, No. 1 (Mar. 1985), pp. 143–68.

INDEX

Figures in **bold** refer to illustrations.

Aerial, Operation 6
aerial battles 58–68, 85–87
Aïn El Turk Cemetery, Oran 80, **92**
aircraft
    British
        Blackburn Skua 42, 58–59, **60**, **64–65**, 66
        Fairey Swordfish 42, **42**, **62**, 80, **82–83**, 84, **85**
    French
        Bréguet 521: **64–64**, 66
        Curtiss H-75: 59, **59**, 58
        Farman F.233: **7**
        Glenn-Martin 167: 77, **77**
        Lioré et Olivier LeO 451: 87, **87**
        Lioré et Olivier LeO H-257: **75**, 77
        Loire 130: 66
Alexander, First Lord of the Admiralty Albert 12, 16
Alexandria, Egypt 6, 71–73, 79–89
Algiers **44**
Anglo-American partnership 91
Anglo-French Union proposed 8–9
Anglo-German Naval Agreement 1935: 26
appeasement efforts, early British 23–25
Armistice, French–Italian 15
armour, ships' 31
Arnauld de la Perière, Konteradmiral Lothar von **12**

Badouin, Paul **9**
Baldwin, Stanley 24
Baudouin, Paul 75
Boudier, Sous-Lieutenant Paul 59, **86**
Bourragué, Contre-Amiral Célestin 44
Bouxin, Contre-Amiral Jacques Félix Emmanuel 47
break out from Mer el-Kébir 53–57
  see also Ships, French, Strasbourg
Brest, France 6, 11, **11–12**
British Expeditionary Force (BEF) 6
Brokensha, Sub-Lieutenant Guy W. 59–60, **60**, 62–63, **64–65**, 66
Brooke, Lieutenant-General Alan 6
Bruen, Lieutenant John M. 58–60, 62–63
burials of French 80, **92**

Cagliari, Sardinia 87
Campbell, Sir Ronald 9, 79–89
Canastel channel, Cap 53–56

Casualties 59, 79–80, **92**
Catapult, Operation (attack on Force de Raid) 20–21, 30–33, 42–43, 46–63, **54–55**
  orders 35–37
  plan 37–39
  opening salvoes 46
  ceasefires offered 53
  aftermath 90–93
  see also Force de Raid
Cayol, Vice-Amiral Lucien 70
Chamberlain, Neville 24–25, **25**
Chatterley, Naval Airman H. T. 59
Cherbourg, France 6, 10–11
Chopin, Lieutenant-Colonel Marcel Edouard 87
Christian, Lieutenant J. 80, 86
chronology of operations 20–22
Churchill, Winston 4–9, **5**, 15–16, 23–25, **24**, 35–36, 71–72, 78, 91
Ciano, Count Galeazzo 92
Collinet, Capitaine de Vaisseau Louis 46–47, 68, **68**, 75
commanders, opposing 23–28
communications issues 9, 12, 43, 73
Cunningham, Vice Admiral Sir Andrew 6, 8, 35, **36**, 71–73

Daladier, Édouard 27
Danbé, Capitaine de Vaisseau Jules Julien Lucien Henri **41**
Darlan, Amiral François 5–10, 12–15, **17**, 18–19, 26–28, **28**, 44–45, 73, 92–93, **93**
De Gaulle, Général Charles 19
De Laborde, Amiral Jean 93
De Montgolfier, Adjutant Paul 62
defences at Mers el-Kébir and Oran **38**, 38–39
demolition teams 37
Derrien, Contre-Amiral Edmond Louis Hyacinthe 43
disposition of Marine Nationale prior to operations **32**
Dodecanese Islands 6
Dufay, Lieutenant de Vaisseau Bernard 40–41
Duff Cooper, Alfred 17
Dunbar-Nasmith, Admiral Martin 70
Duplat, Vice-Amiral Émile 5
Durand-Viel, Vice-Amiral Georges 27
Duval, Lieutenant de Vaisseau **64–65**, 66

Eisenhower, Lieutenant General Dwight D. 93

escape of French ships from Atlantic coast 10–12
Estéva, Vice-Amiral Jean-Pierre 16, 75, 78

Force de Raid (Mers el-Kébir) 8, 28, 42-43, **40**
  see also Catapult, Operation
Force X (Alexandria) 6, 71–73
forces, opposing 29–33
Franco, General Francisco 10
Frossard, Capitaine de Frégate Louis 63

Gensoul, Vice-Amiral Marcel-Bruno 16–17, 28, 40–42, **41**, 44, 53, **92**
Gibraltar 75–77
Gisclon, Chief Sergeant 86
Godfrey-Faussett, Lieutenant D. 80
Godfroy, Vice-Amiral René-Émile 6, 12, 71–73
gold reserves, movement of French 18
Gort, General Lord 17
Griffith, Midshipman A. 86
guns, calibres of 31–33

Habibas Islands, North Africa 80
Halifax, Canada 18
Halifax, Viscount 23, **24**
Hebrard, Sous-Lieutenant Paul Marcel 62, 86
Hériard-Dubreuil, Capitaine Marc 87
Hitler, Adolf 13, **14**, 92, 93
Hodgkinson, Lieutenant Commander Guy B. 67, 79–81
Holland, Captain Cedric 40–42, 44, **45**
Hoth, General der Infanterie Hermann 6
Hughes, Commandant Marcel 60
Huntziger, Général d'armée Charles 13

Jarry, Contre-Amiral Marcel Louis Hippolyte 43

Keitel, Generaloberst Wilhelm 15

La Sénia airfield 44, 60, 87
Le Luc, Vice-Amiral Maurice 7, 43–44
Le Pivain, Capitaine de Vaisseau Louis René Edmond 47, 51
Legrand, Sergeant Legrand André 62
Lemelsen, General der Panzertruppen Joachim 6

Lever, Operation (attack on *Dunkerque*) 79–89, **82–83**, 84, **88–89**
Leygues, Georges 26
Lila, Unternehmen (Operation) 93, **93**
Lloyd, Lord George 12–13
London Naval Treaty 1930 26–27

Marine Nationale 25–26, 32
Médiouna airfield 77
mines, magnetic 42–43
Monraisse, Capitaine Hubert 62, **86**
Morlat, Commandant Jules 60
Munich Agreement 1938: 27
Murtin, Commandant Jacques-Louis 60
Mussolini, Benito 26–27

Newson, Captain Alan 79, 81, **85**
Noguès, Général d'armée Charles 17
North, Vice Admiral Dudley 8, 16–17, 34–35

Oran, North Africa 8, **43**, 56
orders of battle 33

Pennès, Général Roger 60–62
Pétain, Maréchal Philippe 8–9, **9**
plans, opposing 37–39
Plymouth, Devon 70–71
Portalis, Capitaine Gérard 59, 85–86, **86**
Pound, First Sea Lord Sir Dudley 12, 16, **28**

Raeder, Großadmiral Erich 13–14, **14**
Regia Marina 26–27
Reichenau, Generalfeldmarschall Walter von **12**
Relizane airfield 60
retaliation by French forces 73–77, **74, 76**
Rethondes, Armistice of 7–9, 13–16
Reynaud, Paul 4–5, **5**, 8, **9**
Riddler, Petty Officer Thomas F. 59
Robert, Amiral Georges 18
Rommel, Generalmajor Erwin 6
Roosevelt, Franklin D. 7, 91
Rougevin-Baville, Colonel Alfred André 60
Rousseau-Dumarcet, Capitaine Louis 60

Saint-Denis-du-Sig airfield 60, 86
Sales, Sergeant Edouard 62
Seguin, Capitaine de Vaisseau Henri 80, 85
ships
British
Active, HMS (destroyer) 31
Arethusa, HMS (cruiser) 30, 46
Ark Royal, HMS (aircraft carrier) 29–30, 40–41, **42**, 58–59, 80
Devonshire, HMS (heavy cruiser) 18
Dunedin, HMS (light cruiser) 18
Enterprise, HMS (cruiser) 30, 46
Escort, HMS (destroyer) 30
Faulknor, HMS (destroyer) 30
Fearless, HMS (destroyer) 30
Foresight, HMS (destroyer) 30
Forester, HMS (destroyer) 30
Foxhound, HMS (destroyer) 30, 40–41, **42**
Hood, HMS (battleship) 29–31, 33, **37**, 46, **56**
Keppel, HMS (destroyer) 31
Neptune, HMS (light cruiser) 12
Orion, HMS (light cruiser) 12
Pandora, HMS (submarine) 75
Resolution, HMS (battleship) 29–31, 33, 46
Sydney, HMS (light cruiser) 12
Thames, HMS (submarine) 71
Valiant, HMS (battleship) 30–31, 33, 46
Vidette, HMS (destroyer) 31
Vortigern, HMS (destroyer) 31
Wrestler, HMS (destroyer) 31, 53, 63, **64–65**, 66
French
Algérie (cruiser) 5, **6**
Basque (destroyer) 6
Bretagne (battleship) 8, 31, **46–47**, 47–51, **48–50**, **51**, 53, 90
Colbert (light cruiser) 6
Commandant Teste (seaplane carrier) 47, **51**, 78
Duguay-Trouin (light cruiser) 6, 12
Dunkerque (battleship) 8, **26**, 28–29, 33, 47, **48–49**, 50, 51–53, **52**, 78, 78–86, **82–83**, 84, 90, **91**
Dupleix (light cruiser) 6
Duquesne (heavy cruiser) 6
Émile Bertin (light cruiser) 18, **19**
Estérel (tug) 52
Foch (cruiser) 5, **73**
Forbin (destroyer) 6
Fortuné (destroyer) 6
Gloire (cruiser) 44
Grouin de Cou (patrol boat) 80
Jean Bart (battleship) 8, **16**, 29
Kersaint (destroyer) **52**, 53–54
La Poursuivante (torpedo boat) 68
Le Terrible (destroyer) 53, **57**
Lorraine (battleship) 6, 12, **72**
Lynx (destroyer) 53, 57
Massilia, SS 17, **17**
Mogador (destroyer) 53, **53, 63**, **82–83**, 84, 90
Montcalm (cruiser) **44**
Paris (battleship) 70, **70**
Proteé (submarine) 6
Provence (battleship) 8, 31, **46**, 47, **48–49**, 50, **51, 78**, 90
Richelieu (battleship) 6, 8, 18, 29, **30**, 87
Rigault de Genouilly (colonial sloop) 63, 67, **67**, 75
Sétoise (patrol boat) 80
Strasbourg (battleship) 8, **8**, 28–29, 33, **46**, 47, **48–49**, 50, 57–70, **58–59**, 75, 90, **93**
Suffren (heavy cruiser) 6, 12
Surcouf (submarine cruiser) 71, **71**
Terre-Neuve (patrol boat) 80–81, **81**, **82–83**, 84, **85**, 91
Tigre (destroyer) 53, 57
Tomade (destroyer) 43
Tourville (heavy cruiser) 6
Tramontane (destroyer) **43**
Typhon (destroyer) **43**
Victor Schoelcher (cargo vessel) **18**
Volta (destroyer) 53, 57
Waldeck-Rousseau (cruiser) 30
Somerville, Vice-Admiral Sir James 25, 34–42, **35**, 56, 78–79
Sprague, Commander Denis 71
Supreme War Council, Anglo-French 4–5

Torch, Operation 93
Toulon, France 35–36, 93, **93**
Tours, France 4–5
Treaty of Versailles 26
Trémolet, Sous-Lieutenant René 62

units, German ground 6, **93**
Unity Declaration, British and French 7

Vado, Operation 5–6, **6**
Vuillemin, Général Joseph 62

Washington Naval Treaty 1922: 26–27
Wells, Vice Admiral Lionel 58
Weygand, Général Maxime 4–5, 8–9, **9**, 62
withdrawal of Marine Nationale from north-west France **11**